THE

100

Greatest Ideas for Building the Business of Your Dreams

Ken Langdon

THE

100

Greatest Ideas for Building the Business of Your Dreams

Ken Langdon

CAPSTONE

First published 2000 by
Capstone Publishing Limited
Oxford Centre for Innovation
Mill Street
Oxford OX2 0JX
United Kingdom
http://www.capstone.co.uk

British Library Cataloguing in Publication Data
A CIP catalogue record for this book is available from the British Library

ISBN 1-84112-033-2

Typeset in 11/14 pt Plantin by
Sparks Computer Solutions Ltd, Oxford
http://www.sparks.co.uk
Printed and bound by
T.J. International Ltd, Padstow, Cornwall

This book is printed on acid-free paper

Substantial discounts on bulk quantities of Capstone books are available to corporations, professional associations and other organisations. For details telephone Capstone Publishing on (+44-1865-811113) or fax (+44-1865-240941).

Contents

Six Greatest Ideas for Becoming a Consultant 29

Four Greatest Ideas for Working from the Office of Your Dreams 37

Five Greatest Ideas for Financing Your Business 41

Six Greatest Ideas for Selling Big Ticket Items – Business to Business

Five Greatest Ideas for Managing Your Bank

Five Greatest Ideas for Running the Board Effectively

Ten Greatest Ideas for Building the Retail Business of Your Dreams

Ten Greatest Quick Tips for Building the Dream

Six Greatest Ideas for Building Creative Plans

127

Eight Greatest Ideas for Growing by Acquisition

143

Three Greatest Ideas for Building the Empire of Your Dreams

151

*A*cknowledgements

I am very grateful to the many people who gave me their opinions, taking valuable time out from their heavy 'business building' schedules. I have listed them at the back. Mark, Richard and Simon at Capstone were enormously helpful and, of course, were responsible to a huge extent for the *100 Greatest* project happening at all.

My thanks also to Matthew Bates, Julie Wright, Julie Macleod and Paula Bates from WHSmith for their part in the project.

Introduction

A lot of people work in environments where they have little job satisfaction or are just plain unhappy. They may be bored with doing the same job for a long time. They may have become tired of the eccentricity, and occasional ludicrousness, of big companies beset with internal politics and meetings, bloody meetings. They may feel threatened by the sense that their skills are less necessary than they were to the company and that any time now they may be invited to spend more time with their families. This negative force sets them thinking about becoming their own master, telling the boss what they can do with their job and going on their own.

On the positive side, they look with some envy at people who have set up their own businesses, stopped making someone else rich and started to make money the best way – using someone else's labour. They may have had to work hard to achieve it and had some scares on the way, but they have made it. They report to no-one, they work when they want, they make the rules and, who knows, they may even have an exit strategy by which they sell the business and end with a whole lot more pension money than two-thirds of final salary.

Employees also look positively at another kind of self-employed person. These people do not seem as hassled as the first lot. They seem to have settled for a comfortable standard of living rather than risking all for luxury but it still looks a better life style than the rat race in Megacorp Inc. They work on their own, they work when they like, dress casually, seem to be able to fit in more golf, and use the phrase 'seeing more of one's family' positively rather than as a threat. They too have taken risks, but their sights are lower in business terms, although possibly not if you measure happiness in some quality-of-life way.

What exactly is the business of your dreams? Let's say that in the future, either sooner or later, you want to sell a business to new shareholders as an investment and by so doing leave yourself able to spend more time with your family in a state of blissful financial independence; or you want to become famous; or you just want to improve the way you live. Whichever is the case, the time to start planning is now. Even if you have plenty of time before getting out of your current organisation, you need to think about the skills and experience you will need when the great day comes. If, however, your dream is to stay in a big company and prosper, then you need to learn how to build your part of the enterprise into a thriving entity by building it up and up.

If you have already started on the route, then you need the distilled wisdom of many people to help you to your dream. This book does that. I have spoken to many successful people during the writing of this book and gratefully acknowledge their help at the back.

Seven Greatest Ideas for Taking the Plunge

Introduction

I know it is an old cliché, taking the plunge, but it is the most apposite phrase to use when you are contemplating emerging from gainful employment with an employer who looks after most of your material needs and starting up the business of your dreams. Apposite because it is scary the first time you do it, you know there is going to be a cold shock as you hit the water and of course people do drown. The other similarity is standing on the diving board looking down. Shall I, shan't I?

Here are some ideas proposed as, in the main, things you can do before you leap. From understanding the need for short- and long-term thinking, *Idea 1*, to literally buying yourself out of a big company – *Idea 5*.

Idea 1 – Know that two heads are better than one

Later in this section you will have the opportunity of assessing your own suitability for being on your own, but I have first to report from observation and from conversations with people who have done it very successfully that the top person in a new and growing company needs to have two heads, either literally or metaphorically.

The problem is the old one of balancing the pressures of today against the longer-term thinking required to build the dream, and it looks like this:

1. Without a long-term strategy companies run the risk that decisions they are making today will have a negative impact on results in the future.

2. But we have to stay real; business people are always under pressure to carry out urgent day-to-day tasks. They have to meet today's objectives and overcome short-term problems. They have to respond to their customers, whoever they are. Everyone is involved in such work and in operational, or short-term, planning. In a fast-moving environment it is little wonder that planning for the future tends to take second place.

3. If these two statements are true for all organisations, they are much more dramatically experienced in start-ups and small companies. There is no point in defending an action as being right for the long term if it is going to assist the business to run out of cash. On the other hand, making a sale that is outside the main route you have planned could be catastrophic for the future.

So we come back to the two heads. The top of any start-up company needs a 'can do' and 'do it now' attitude. It needs someone who will discuss a problem find a solution and immediately pick up the telephone to start implementing the solution. As for the solutions themselves, expect to need some fancy footwork just to keep the business afloat. No one has solved the particular problems you are about to face; there is no precedent, so one of the two heads has to spot solutions or activities that would be described by some managers in large companies as completely off the wall.

And yet, and yet, no one built a business without thought for the future affecting what we do now – the second head.

Some people can simulate the two heads inside their one brain. Reacting, ducking and weaving with the best of them but also from time to time checking that they are not mortgaging the future or taking short-term measures that endanger the long-term goal. Others form teams of two where one person is clearly the go-getter, and the other the 'just a minute, let's think this through.' So, think on. Can you do it yourself with a Chinese wall in your head separating the two processes, or do you need a partner?

Idea 2 – Choose an arbiter or an assertive mentor

Suppose you have decided to go with two people, the next decision is whether the partnership is equal or if one of the partners is slightly more equal than the other. Some venture capitalists who have worked with many start-ups have come to the conclusion that every team needs an identified leader. They advocate, for example, that in a limited company the shares are not split 50/50 but one shareholder is given the edge, even if it is only 51/49. That way, they claim, if it becomes necessary to arbitrate between two courses of action they both know in advance whose opinion will hold.

But some successful entrepreneurs, whose experience is that the 50-50 split can work well, dispute this. One such, the long-term thinker of the duo, says that even the smallest edge would have lessened his ability to argue his case, and the 'do it now' merchant would have forced through mistakes. He went on, however, to reveal that there was an arbiter, or at least another person involved in the decision-making process. This person played the role of non-executive, and low-paid, chairman. During planning sessions, *Idea 85*, the chairman would force the two people through a route of logic that would often reveal to the more impetuous of the two that the way forward he was advocating was not right for the business as a whole. Indeed this became such a feature of the behaviour of the team that he would often, at the end of such a discussion, turn on his partner in mock rage saying 'There you are, I told you it wasn't a good idea' – his way of backing down.

If you are doing the whole thing on your own, make sure you have built in at least a simulation of this arbitration. It doesn't matter who it is, your accountant, your spouse, your eldest child or your bank manager; have someone in whom you confide and who can tell you to your face that you are about to drop a clanger. (On second thoughts probably not your bank manager. As we will see, they are more concerned with avoiding trouble and potential bad debts than encouraging the green shoots of commerce. If the business takes three years really to get going and prosper, they will have moved on before it happens.) Robert Townsend, the ex-CEO of Avis had a wife who helped with this role, as well as an ally in the senior ranks of the business. His wife famously made him think about his role as the director of strategic planning in one of his companies by saying – 'And what did you plan today dear?' His feisty sidekick on being told of a rather hairy diversification Townsend was proposing said, 'I don't know what you call that, but we Pollacks call it pissing in the soup.'

Idea 3 – Be quite clear what your dream is

The best advice you can get from successful people who have done it is the source of much of this book. All of them are agreed on one thing – don't mix up your objectives. Take, for example, advice on the type of person to hire into your business; it is quite different depending on your objective. If you are trying to build the 'best' or the 'biggest', you will have to hire really good people and take on board the problems such people inevitably bring with them. If your concern is to live the way you want unfettered by outsiders' demands, you no more want the hassles of the creative and bright than you want a heron on your goldfish pond.

Eventually the options boil down to three:

- *Money.* Some people simply want to be rich. They want to make a lot of money as quickly as possible and then retire early to spend more time with their grown-up families than they ever did when they were young. To do this, they have to build a dream business with apparent shareholder value that they can sell in, probably, an earn-out allowing them to do another three years in the business before retiring as one of the richest five hundred in the land. The decisions that such people take will be as consistent as possible with the well-being of the business as such, but the over-riding objective is their personal wealth and they will take risks with the business in that regard. As one of them so neatly put it, 'OK, maybe we are growing a bit too fast for the theorists, but I don't want to have to dig my own swimming pool.'

Often charming, sometimes simply frightening, these people know exactly what they want and will work hard and do whatever is necessary to make that happen. Don't, incidentally, get in their way if you are a 'quiet life' person.

Their strengths include their enthusiasm and their ability to understand instantly the way they should take their business forward – the aiming point is easy to identify. The successful ones discover new insights in how to manage a business for owner's profit, and everyone can learn from them.

- *Fame.* Other people want to build a business to make a name for themselves. They will happily appear in their own advertisements and punt themselves as gurus to the broadcasters and press at any opportunity. They desire a high profile, an OBE at least and eventually seats on government agencies that pay very little or nothing but give them cocktail party access to the great and the good. They too will work hard and do what is necessary to fulfil their dream. Their strengths include their unquenchable self-belief and single-mindedness. Add to that the amount of free publicity they can generate to advance their businesses and you can see the connection between their ambition and their companies' success. If they have a weakness, it can be suspicion and fear of other talented people in the business, whom they think might eclipse their reputation as being, in fact '*the* person in the one-person business.' I knew one who declared that he wanted inscribed on the tombstone above his grave the epitaph 'He was the founder of Esprit' (Esprit being the name of his company). I forbore from telling him that his attitude to his senior people that he had messed up on the way, was likely to make them search that grave out so that they could dance on it.

- *Lifestyle.* Some people tire of the rat race and want to get out to build a more suitable lifestyle. As we have said, that ambition will change dramatically how they run their businesses. Their personal lives are completely mixed in with their business lives, and decision-making on the latter will always start from the former. Often they are fulfilling their lifelong passion or hobby and turning it into a business that will probably not put them up with the mega-rich, and certainly not make them feature in the national press, but that is not their dream, and that is not how they define success.

So, which are you? All three objectives obey the attributes of a good objective, namely:

- *measurable* – they will know when they have reached the dream;
- *achievable* – many people have succeeded before them and often not the most likely people (in fact, by following common-sense rules you really can build the business of your dreams); and
- *time targeted* – you have to know when you want to get there, because we are a long time dead.

But most of all they are specific and clear. They give the aiming point and thus define the opening, middle and end games. So take a moment to decide what you want to do, and then read on to discover, from a combination of peoples' experiences and sound business practices, how to get there.

Idea 4 – Know thyself

This was the motto above the oracle at Delphi and gives good advice. From the attributes people have discussed with me as important, I have put together this simple self-assessment scheme to give a clear indication as to whether or not you are a suitable case for joining the ranks of the small-business person or entrepreneur. How well do the following attributes describe you?

Fill in the following. Answer the questions with:
1 Yes   2 Mainly   3 Not really   4 No

	1	2	3	4
I am a good listener	1	(2)	3	4
I hate putting things off	1	2	(3)	4
I tackle hard jobs before easy ones	1	(2)	3	4
The family supports my decision to set up on my own	(1)	2	3	4
I am ready to work all day, every day when necessary	(1)	2	3	4
I have good self discipline	1	(2)	3	4
I can sell	1	(2)	3	4
I like selling	1	(2)	3	4
I take decisions carefully	1	2	(3)	4
I deal well with stress	1	(2)	3	4
I learn from my mistakes	(1)	2	3	4
I take advice	1	(2)	3	4
I can motivate people	(1)	2	3	4
I can think long term	1	(2)	3	4
I enjoy working on my own	1	2	(3)	4
I hate office politics getting in the way of company objectives	(1)	(2)	3	4
I can do without the trappings of big companies – for example, kick off meetings, award ceremonies, company sponsorship and parties	(1)	2	3	4
I like to be in control	(1)	(2)	3	4
I prefer to work to objectives rather than carry out tasks	1	2	3	4
I understand the risks of going on my own	(1)	2	3	4

7   20   9
16
36

Analysis

Add up your score by totalling the numbers in the boxes you have marked.

- *Score 70–80*
  You are not by your own estimation the type to go plunging in to a small entrepreneurial business. Read this book as a guide to building your dream empire within a large organisation.
- *Score 50–70*
  Hmm. You have some of the traits of a plunger but have another look at the areas where you scored 3 or 4 and ask yourself if you could improve with practice. If the answer to that is yes, then have a go by all means but be prepared for a few sleepless nights.
- *Score 30–50*
  Go on, go for it. You don't enjoy the big company that much and think of the benefits
- *Score 20–30*
  What are you waiting for, stupid? You are a natural. You should have done it years ago so come on in, the water's *terrifying*.

Hang on, you have only done the easy part of 'Know thyself.' Now ask your nearest and dearest, and then some trustworthy colleagues, to agree or disagree with your own assessment.

Idea 5 – Ease yourself out by MBO

Large companies tend to follow fashions. The eighties were famous for diversification, with directors looking at businesses with no connection to the existing one and flinging their shareholders' money around to buy them. They ended up with huge conglomerates where it became harder and harder to see what value membership of the morass of businesses that made up the whole added to each individual business. Recession struck and 'core business' became the order of the day. This involved selling off those chunks of the business not seen as strategic and which happened to be, quite honestly, those chunks that were demonstrably not making money. If your company has a board-level strategy of doing this, you have an opportunity to go on your own in the same business you have built for someone else by *man-agement buyout* – MBO.

One of the best examples of this was the empire grown by Saatchi and Saatchi in the advertising business. They bought up many small agencies for sums of money that were only just relevant when the economy was booming and highly unrealistic when the downturn came along. Many founders of businesses prospered twice in this regime, once when they sold the business to Saatchi in the first place, and again when they bought it back for a fraction of that price two or three years later.

Large businesses frequently have around them such millstones of illogic and strategic madness that taking a division from them and turning it round into a profitable concern is often desperately easy.

I offer this illustration to remind us at this stage that large businesses frequently have around them such millstones of illogic and strategic madness that taking a division from them and turning it round into a profitable concern is often desperately easy. Here is proof of this by one specific example and one generalisation. Both of these examples show that the proposer of an MBO has one distinct advantage over the people running the large company. The proposer is concerned with the detail of the business they are about to run whereas their quarry, the managers in the Megacorps, have more strategic things on their minds – like their careers.

In one instance an advertising agency offered a small agency owner a deal. He could back his agency into a new company they were forming as part of the large organisation they were building. He would then take over as CEO of the new company containing his agency and three others they were buying. The price was dependent on an 'earn-out'. If his original business grew to a certain profit target, they would pay a large amount of money. What they didn't think about, and the small businessman realised immediately, was that taking his salary out of the costs of his original business and transferring it to the new entity put him half way to achieving the profit growth target at a stroke. Neat eh?

Now consider this. When you are dealing with a large organisation with a view to taking one of their less prosperous bits off their hands, you are looking at it as *TICK – think in cash, knucklehead Idea 55*. However, the manager of the bit you are buying is thinking in terms of his or her management accounting system. In most big organisations, for example, head office does not allow that its own costs, which are apportioned to the divisions, must make some sort of contribution or be cut. Here is what happens if head office believes that its costs are inevitable and fixed.

In this case head office costs of £24 million are allocated to divisions by turnover.

Division	A	B	C	Total
Turnover	100	50	50	200
Divisional contribution	18	7	5	30
HO costs	12	6	6	24
Profit	6	1	(1)	6

The long-term viability of division C is plainly not there and the decision is taken regretfully to sell or close the division. By definition head office costs are unaffected in total and need to be re-allocated.

Division	A	B	Total
Turnover	100	50	150
Divisional contribution	18	7	25
HO costs	16	8	24
Profit	2	(1)	1

Oh dear, now division B faces the chop.

Division	A	Total
Turnover	100	100
Divisional contribution	18	18
HO costs	24	24
Profit	(6)	(6)

Good isn't it? By refusing to believe that head office costs should be directly linked to the contribution of the divisions, we are forced, once again with great regret, logically to close the business. Many MBOs get a head start from this kind of nonsense. One of the people I talked to while writing this book bought a division from a big multinational. According to its accounting system the division lost £500,000 the previous year. The entrepreneur bought it for £250,000 and it produced profits of £500,000 the following year without his doing much at all. Simply put, the management accounting systems were giving a totally wrong reading of the state of health of the division.

It depends, of course, on the board strategy but most boards nowadays are interested in anything that offers demonstrable shareholder value. This makes them highly amenable to a well thought out bid by middle managers to buy out part of the business. Could this work for you?

Idea 6 – Research is not optional

Before you take the plunge, it pays to have a good look at the situation you are getting yourself into. This used to be difficult. You used to have to hire some arrogant information company to give you the fruits of the interviews and document researched information on the prospected market, competition and so on. Nowadays it is much easier. Take competitive research. As long as you know the names of the key competitors you can plug into their Website and hey presto they will volunteer 80–90% of the data you need. The same goes for the market, with millions of words of research data available either free of charge or at very low cost.

So there is no excuse now for plunging uninformed. Do not rely totally on the Internet, of course; remember to look at the physical side of the business world as well. Go and look at where your competitors and customers work. Check out the environment you will have to work in and so on.

It may seem a bit upside-down, but in order to make sure you are gathering the information you require, here is the checklist of a successful small business man projecting himself about three years down the road to the business of his dreams. 'What you will want to have positive answers to', he said, 'are the following questions:

- Who exactly are my customers?
- Do I like working with these people?
- Have I built an effective network with my customers and suppliers?
- Does the work integrate with my preferred lifestyle?
- Are the people I have gathered around me like-minded individuals?
- Am I building something that has real value?
- Do I add real value?'

You will find that this checklist firstly guides you in your research and, secondly, makes sure that the business you are contemplating will still be a dream in three years' time and not have turned into a horrible nightmare.

Idea 7 – Feel free – franchise

This is a sort of mezzanine floor diving board, with the not inconsiderable advantage that far fewer new franchise businesses fail than single start-up companies. (The statistics on business failures are too depressing, so we will ignore them. No one got rich worrying about following a historic trend.) You also get a head start with your marketing, assuming you are taking on a franchise that is well set. This pretty much guarantees some customers, but just how many you will have to research.

Be very careful with the market and turnover predictions from the franchiser. There have been a lot of instances where these have been hopelessly optimistic, showing cashflow predictions for a number of existing sites, and projecting them on to new sites where possibly there are never going to be the sales available.

Beware also being rushed into a franchise. The franchiser people with whom you are dealing are themselves targeted with getting new people on board as quickly as possible. They will give you all sorts of good reasons for speed including the one about someone else being very interested, but you must take your time and complete your research. Be sceptical too about the franchiser's view on experience. People I have spoken to all believe that it is dangerous to go straight into a retail franchise, for example, if you have no experience at all of how retail businesses are managed. Oh, and this is one of the times in business where doing things without a lawyer who understands the area you are going into would be reckless. Pay the money and get good advice.

Finally, check that it will be your dream in a few years' time. You will not be fully independent and what feels like help and assistance at the start, may feel like interference further down the road. Remember too that if one of your fellow franchisees anywhere in the world makes a mistake and poisons a couple of customers, you will bear the backlash. But the amount of capital you require is low and results can be quick, so it is worth looking at it, particularly if you feel you need to cushion the shock of hitting the water.

Ten Greatest Ideas for Planning Your Business

Introduction

I am going to avoid the frequent use of the word 'strategy' in this section. All businesses have a strategy, and yours can be no exception; but we need say no more at this stage than agree a simple definition of the word. From there we can pass on to the much more detailed concept of building a short-term (say one- or two-year) business plan. This will contain the basic ideas for the business, and then move to the detailed figures that you need for a number of reasons:

- They give you the aiming point by calculating the point at which sales exceed costs, *plan for a lucky break-even Idea 17*.
- They give you the data you require to survive the interview with the banker that you will need to go through if you want to borrow now or in the future, *take the banking forms seriously Idea 16*.
- Getting down to figures is the ultimate proof that you have really thought the thing through.
- However brilliant your idea is and you are at implementing it, you will have to get used to talking about and dealing with numbers and money – so start now.

But we have to sail over the hurdle marked 'strategy' first. Whatever anyone tells you, a business strategy is a statement of what you are going to sell, to whom you are going to sell it to and how you are going to go about that selling process. If I add that the third element 'how' will also demonstrate what you believe is, or will be, your competitive edge or unique selling proposition, then we have said all that needs to be said about strategy. If you want more, there is a longer, although still pretty short, version of this in *The 100 Greatest Ideas for Building your Career*, Langdon, Capstone, 2000.

So now let's get on with the details.

Idea 8 – Choose your markets wisely

However obvious this may seem, spend a bit of time in considering who will buy your products and services. Now try and group them in some way. It may make sense to think about large and small customers, or ones that are nationwide, and those who only operate close to home. Only you can organise a sensible grouping. A contractor in the building trade, for example, may think about their customers as:

- end-user customers;
- consultants such as architects; and
- other contractors and sub-contractors.

The point of this grouping is to identify later on in the process where greater opportunities lie and where better margins and profits can be found. This may mean that you will start off looking for the easiest business just to get some sales, but with an emphasis in your selling and marketing on another market group who, once you have cracked into it, will give you better profits or larger contracts.

Even at this stage there is a point to dreaming a bit. It may seem far-fetched to consider a major nationwide builder as a prospect at this time, but who knows in the future? Write it down; once a great idea is documented it can never be lost. Remember while you are at this planning stage that dreams are about the unknown as well as the known. Indeed it is axiomatic that following your dreams will take you in unexpected directions.

A lot of small businesses start on the back of one customer. If this is the case with yours, don't let that be an excuse for missing out this section of the plan or for doing it perfunctorily. Things change and you should be aware of the main direction in which you want changes to occur. You are going to do the figures on the first year of trading, but it is not a bad idea to think two or even three years ahead in terms of the markets that you may have a go at.

Idea 9 – Use the 'ideal' technique to understand your customers

Customers have always traded product or service features against the price they are prepared to pay. They also look for how well your business processes provide customer satisfaction and the relationships they build with the people that they meet from your organisation. To build long-term customer loyalty you need to understand their buying criteria – what questions will they use to compare you with your competitors? To understand this thoroughly you have to talk to as many customers or potential customers as you can. What are they looking for? How do they make their decisions to buy?

Now you need to assess what your customers would say was their view of the ideal offering in each of the following four areas – product, process, people and price. Again you can ask them for their opinion of what would be best for them, either in a meeting or a telephone call, or by inviting them to join part of a planning session. The points they make are their buying criteria and will fit into one of the four factors mentioned above. Customers will tell you what ideally they want from you if you ask the right questions. You may not be able to achieve the ideal the customer is searching for, but if you know what it is you should come close.

Not all the criteria will have the same importance to a customer, so the final step in this technique is to put a priority against each criterion. When you have finished defining the buying criteria and the customer's ideal, think about their relative importance on a scale of 1–10. You do not want, when it comes to making decisions about what your offering is going to be, to work hard on issues which the customer thinks less significant, if it means putting less effort into issues which they believe to be vital. These priorities will therefore have an impact on product, process, people and price decisions later in the planning process. Chart the result of this work on a matrix.

Customer value statement

Criteria group	Criteria	Customer ideal	Priority
Product or service *What you supply to your customer*	e.g. quality, or ease of use	e.g. zero faults	7
Process *How you deal with your customer*	e.g. ease of ordering	e.g. standard contract for all items	3
People *The quality of the people who deal with the customer*	e.g. after-sales support	e.g. single-number help desk	6
Price *The cost of the product or service to the customer*	e.g. competitive	e.g. lowest price available	7

Idea 10 – Know thine enemy

If you have a lot of competitors you may have to choose a few key ones to analyse. There are many sources of competitive information. You should obtain your competitors' brochures and promotional material to understand what they believe are their strengths and how they present them to customers. Relevant trade journals have comparisons of products and reviews of things that are new. If it is sufficiently important, you can buy reports of competitive comparisons from market analysts. Your customers and prospects can also be a source of competitive knowledge as can people who join your organisation from a competitor. Now relate this information to your customer by making a chart of your competitors' ability to meet the decision criteria of your customers, using the customer value matrix. You should note where they are nearer to the customer's ideal than you are.

Most organisations see their current competitors as providers of similar products or services. In fact this is not the case. There is often another way of doing things. If, for example, you intend to run a helicopter service carrying business people out to remote islands, a current competitor may be another contractor offering to run the same route. It is possible that future competitors may be video-conferencing companies who would render the journey unnecessary. Think about what your customers require and what other ways they could meet their needs apart from using your types of products and services. Think widely about competitive possibilities, because it is certain that there are other organisations thinking widely about their prospects in your chosen markets.

Think widely about competitive possibilities, because it is certain that there are other organisations thinking widely about their prospects in your chosen markets.

The market does not stand still – nor do your competitors. What a customer found interesting and satisfying for even a long time in the past will not last for ever. Whole organisations have in the past been caught out because a product feature introduced by a competitor has become desirable and even fashionable. You have to be ready for such a change, or to react quickly if you did not anticipate the event. You should try to be in the position of the person who first brought out the new feature.

Look, in the end you are going to have to explain to customers and prospects why they should prefer your offering to other people's. So work it out now, and keep working at it until you have convinced yourself.

Idea 11 – Describe and compare the key people

If you are going to build a business, you will almost certainly have to attract some key people who will help you go for the dream. Make sure you have agreed their role and their responsibilities. Check that their experience is entirely relevant to that role and examine their network. Every person who joins you should bring their own contacts and business network that will help you in expanding sales. Write that down along with their qualifications and skills. If you do this for everyone including yourself, you will have a concise record of the starting point of the skills in the business. Their current salary will be a starting point for the costing exercise to come later.

Idea 12 – Reach your market realistically

Most small businesses get started by the owner speaking to the first customer, then the second customer and so on. But at some point, depending on the industry you are in, you may have to spend money on promotions, advertising mailshots, etc. It is a good idea to be wary of the company brochure. If you are cold calling prospects on the telephone for instance, you will frequently be asked to 'send the brochure'. In my experience nothing comes of this, and it is better to continue the conversation by explaining that a general brochure is not helpful, since all your sales start from understanding the needs of your customers. Ask them if you can come and see them to discuss it, at which point you will be able to send a letter tailored to their requirements rather than a catch-all brochure.

This approach is a good sieve. If the person agrees to see you, you are making progress, if they do not, then their request for a brochure was simply a polite way of ending the telephone call. It is, of course, a faith position; but I do not believe in company brochures, they are no substitute for selling a particular item to a particular customer.

At this planning stage look at what your competitors do in terms of advertising, and assess what it would cost to match them. Then decide whether that is a good idea in your first year before adding it to the estimated profit and loss account that comes later in the process.

Idea 13 – Make sure the price is right

You must be well aware of the profit margins available in your industry. Work out a pricing policy that makes the best of this and is at the same time competitive. Look at how your customers expect to pay. What credit terms will they want? What can you offer that will be a trade off for getting better terms than usual? Remember that new players have the least flexibility in waiting for money to come in – that is, they are the most strapped for cash. So, if it is you that is new, be innovative in looking for reasons why you should be paid early and at best up front.

Now look at the business process that you will need to have in place to chase your debtors and make them pay as near to the agreed date as you can. Who will do this chasing?

Finally think about the salespeople you are going to employ. These people are key to your early success if you need more than you to do the selling. In the next section on financing your business, I am going to suggest that you do not in the first place use share options as a way of attracting and motivating people. It's your business, so don't give it away. If you accept this advice you are almost certainly going to have some sort of bonus scheme to get the salespeople selling what you want, when you want it sold. This is crucial. If you make it a straight percentage of sales, you could have problems with the price at which sales are made. Most salespeople will happily accept ten per cent of £900 rather than work hard for the ten per cent of the full price of £1000. Giving things away is much easier than selling them. You will have to explain that giving away ten per cent of the selling price is actually giving away 33% of the profit or even more. Work it out if you don't believe me. Here is a product with a low gross margin to illustrate the point.

	At full price	Discounted
Sale	1000	1000
Discounted @ 10%	0	900
Cost of sale	800	800
Selling expenses	50	50
Profit	150	50

The selling price may only have gone down by 10%, but the net profit has dropped by 66%.

I have seen owners of businesses do very well by giving the salespeople incentives to achieve the gross margin – sales price minus the cost of the product or service sold – rather than the sales figure. That way the motivation is to sell at list price. This may be a more expensive sales bonus scheme but could easily earn its costs. If there is no share option to offer the people who are responsible for growing your business then they are going to be expensive. As usual it's a trade off, but there is no point in being in business if you do not sell your products and services at a healthy price – so get it right.

Idea 14 – Picking your spot

You will need premises. If you are looking at a retail opportunity and need a shop, we cover that in *Ideas 67* and *68*. If you need a yard and warehouse space then those ideas will help with that case too. If all you need is an office then start from home and look at *Ideas 23–26*.

If you do need space consider the following:

- What are the terms?
- If it is a renewable lease, how much will it be to renew it?
- If it is rented when is the next rent review?
- What are the business rates?
- What insurance will you need?
- How long will this space last, and would it be better to allow a bit more for expansion?

Remember that premises do not need to be huge and plush to impress people. Some customers will like to support a startup that is using professional but not flashy accommodation. Some of my customers loved visiting me at my office in my home because they found it a bit of a break. The key is professional – put a lick of fresh paint on and keep it tidy.

There are some exceptions to this rule. You must not look second rate or the 'local firm.' If your aiming point is the top league in advertising, you will need to start with enough finance to have good premises from the start.

Idea 15 – Add up the equipment and start-up costs

Whereas 'premises' is a cost item on which a lot of successful startup people would economise, they tend not to do this in the case of equipment. Investing in the latest technology and making full use of it will probably be worth it in the end. Try doing a cost/benefit analysis on it. Look at the alternative and try to cost that as well. If buying a piece of accounting software means that you or your spouse can do the bookkeeping, then think of the saving that will make at your accountants. The more you can do yourself in terms of printing plans in colour, doing your own copying and having your own Web site, the more control you have over your business and the lower are your running costs. It is the running costs becoming fixed that threaten trouble when sales are poor or when you are starting up. Investment now will keep those running costs to a minimum.

Competitively you must play at least a draw in this area. If they can produce drawings on a large-scale flat bed plotter, then so must you. Take into consideration:

- How will you buy it?
- How long will it last (e.g. £1000 spent today on computers will almost certainly require another £1000 in a year to eighteen months)?
- What are the running costs?
- Will you need training expenses to be able to make use of it?

Finish this exercise and you have done the difficult part of the planning process. Now we have to convert these ideas and decisions into financial matrices and cashflows.

Idea 16 – Take the banking forms seriously

Consultants and bank managers have at least one thing in common. Almost all businesspeople tell them that their particular business is different and that they must not use the same parameters to judge their business as they do for others. Consultants and bank mangers therefore spend a lot of time convincing them that whilst to a certain extent that is true – all businesses do have different detailed characteristics – nevertheless no business can ignore the universal issues that any profit-making company has to take into account. No matter how difficult it is in, for example, a service company to calculate and monitor gross margin, the managers of the business must do it. Another truth that people sometimes plead to be different in their environments is the rule that everything in business is negotiable. No one – lawyer, accountant, financial adviser or supplier of anything – works in a vacuum, therefore everything is negotiable.

All this is to defend the generalised forms that banks make their potential business borrowers fill in before they will consider their case. If the ideas in this section seem reasonable preparation work then I have made the point. I have used the headings and order of one of the major banks' startup forms.

We should take them seriously for a number of reasons:

- You need to manage carefully your relationship with the bank, and this is their first taste of the new boy's professionalism.
- Whatever business you are going into, the grand majority of the form is completely relevant.
- Filling them in ensures that you have thought through the points above and then converted them into a profit and loss account and cashflow statement.
- They are comprehensive. If you have filled them all in apart from bits that genuinely do not apply to your business, then you can rest assured you have covered all the angles.
- They are the first and probably the last bit of free consultancy that the bank will give you.

Now don't forget the point about negotiation. If you find it difficult to fill in one set of bank forms, you may not relish the thought of doing two. And yet, that is what you must do if you are to get the best deal. You need to play one off against another. If, for some reason, one turns your case down, then go to a third and try again. You might that way find that you have two offers to compare after all, and you may just find, if the second bank turns you down, that there is a flaw in your plan that you need to address.

Idea 17 – Plan for a lucky break-even

Finally, your business plan should include, certainly for your use, a break-even analysis. If you have collected all the information above you know your fixed costs or overheads and you know your gross margins on each product fairly accurately. Divide the fixed costs by the gross profit margin per unit to find the number of units you need to sell just to break even. Multiply the number of units by the selling price and you have the value of sales you need to cover your overheads with your gross margin. Divide this figure by 12 and you know what level of sales per month you need to make sure that your turnover covers all your fixed and variable costs for a month. Keep updating this, as there will inevitably be changes in all the figures, particularly gross margin.

You can use the same analysis to calculate what level of sales you would require to cover, for example, capital expenditure or taking on more people.

Six Greatest Ideas for Becoming a Consultant

Introduction

Becoming a consultant is a lifestyle objective in the main, although if you get it right, the money can be good as well. Good but limited, because there are only so many days that you can sell. You will not become famous or build the biggest company in the business unless you take on one of the most difficult management tasks of them all – managing other consultants. Many people become consultants in their middle thirties and another load do it later when they take early retirement from large organisations. Be prepared for a rather lonely working life. Around Christmas time your clients will all at some time say, 'Right I have got to go now; we have one of our Christmas parties on today.' And you just go off, brief case in hand back to the office or spare room if that is where you have set up the galactic headquarters of your consultancy.

Be prepared also for a fair amount of stress. If you are in training, for example, you may well run the same type of course or even exactly the same course for many years. You will find this becomes stressful because by the time you have run it say 30 times you will be so familiar with the material that you will find it hard to believe that anyone does not know this stuff already. You also have the stress of selling enough days to make a living, not just the first year when all is exciting and fresh, but also every single year. No one else is accountable for getting you business.

Finally there is a stress in always being the person in charge. You go to the planning meeting and it's 'OK Ken how do we start?' You go to the seminar and it is up to you to lead the move from the coffee room to the classroom and your job to start the whole thing off. Then there are your sales calls that are also up to you. But the benefits are also excellent. You report to nobody. (In fact I suspect after quite a short time you become unemployable.) And you organise your own life. It does not matter when you work. I prefer to work Saturday mornings, for example, when the telephone does not ring, but I never miss a monthly medal on a Thursday or my weekly foursome. (New clients may find this a bit odd, so I don't tell them that golf is the reason every Thursday is a no go area, until I know them well.) So here are some great ideas for plunging in and going on your own as a consultant.

Idea 18 – Don't be worse off

When you become a consultant it is easy to be misled into thinking that the money is really rather good. It is paid gross of tax, and if you work things correctly you may not have to pay any income tax for up to 18 months. This inflates your income significantly. No one, of course, has made your contribution to a pension plan, and it may take a while for you to set one up. Then there are the expenses of being in business on your own. Think of these items. They are only the cash items; there will be depreciation on fixed assets as well:

- rent and rates;
- buildings insurance;
- business and liability insurance;
- light and heat (even if you are working at home, this will cost more);
- cleaning;
- repairs and maintenance;
- printing, postage and stationery;
- telephone;
- motor running expenses;
- bookkeeping fees;
- accountant's fees;
- bank charges and interest;
- books and research; and

- marketing and advertising.

These expenses could easily add up to not far short of £20,000. Therefore if you are replacing a gross salary of £30,000, you need turnover of:

- expenses   £20,000
- salary   £30,000
- pension   £4,500
- total   £54,500

Now consider the number of days you have available to earn that money. After deduction of weekends, holidays and bank holidays there are about 240 days left in the year.

From experience it is very hard to work more than 140 days actually on site as a consultant. This is different from a contractor who can work more or less all 240 days because they are more like employees than consultants. Consultants have marketing to do, sales calls to make, demonstrations to prepare and preparation work to do for most of the days they work and earn fees.

Here then are the required daily rates to support five different salary levels given sales of 140 or 100 days. Make sure you can charge at least these amounts, or you may find yourself worse off as a consultant than as an employee.

Gross salary to be replaced	£30,000	£40,000	£50,000	£75,000	£100,000
Pension	£4,500	£6,000	£7,500	£11,250	£15,000
Expenses	£20,000	£20,000	£20,000	£20,000	£20,000
Total	£54,500	£66,000	£77,500	£106,250	£135,000
Daily rate for 140 days	£389	£471	£554	£759	£964
Daily rate for 100 days	£545	£660	£775	£1,063	£1,350

Idea 19 – See your value from the customer's point of view

For many years I have offered consultancy services from a company that consists only of myself. I am a one-man band. I did a planning job once for a big electricity company. The job was phase one of three phases and we completed it successfully. Indeed my main sponsor was delighted. When it came to phase two, the amount of money at stake meant that according to their purchasing rules they had to go out to tender. My sponsor was pushed towards McKinseys who, at the time, were doing a lot of work at holding board level, as well as inviting me to bid. I was working with two operating company boards.

Now, since they had used my processes for phase one, it made almost no sense at all to change consultants for the second part of the project. I knew this, of course, and decided to go in at the highest price I dared. I really loaded my quote and waited for the reaction. It came through a telephone call from my sponsor. He sounded concerned and embarrassed and I feared the worst. 'Ken,' he said, 'I've got a problem with your price.' 'Oh my God,' I thought, 'I've overcooked it,' and I started stammering about how we could probably take another look at it. He agreed with this and suggested that I took another person onto the project and 'make it more of a team approach'. 'But that will make it more expensive', says I. 'I know, Ken, the problem is you are more than £200,000 lower than the McKinsey quote. I can't take your number in as it is, the purchasing people will laugh you out of court.'

So, I took another guy on and shoved the price up to what was for me a stratospheric height. We got the business and we certainly holidayed well that year.

Daily rates can be an emotional business. Customers who have not done the calculations shown in *Idea 17* do find daily rates high. There are emotional hurdles to get over as well. I think one is the £1000 mark and when my daily rate was approaching this figure I spoke to a colleague in the advertising business and he suggested I soar way above this figure rather than go in at such an emotional rate. With my heart in my mouth I went up from £900 to £1150 in one jump. It worked and my existing customers accepted it. New customers took a different view of me as a £1150 a day person and it did my image no harm at all.

I suppose you can overdo it, but remember what you are bringing to a business in terms of value. If, for example, you are brought in to arbitrate between two opposing camps backing different strategies for the company's way ahead and you manage to find a solution that both sides find acceptable, you may very well have stopped that company from facing difficult resignations or faltering without a sense of direction for a long period of time. Now think of what that piece of work has been worth.

Idea 20 – Know which comes first, the product or the customer

There is no such thing as a product without a market, just as there is no such thing as a market if you do not have a product for it. So, think in terms of 'product markets'.

There is no such thing as a product without a market, just as there is no such thing as a market if you do not have a product for it. So, think in terms of 'product markets'.

When you have been on your own for a while, and particularly if you meet a lot of middle managers in your clients' premises, you will be surprised how many people are thinking of doing the same as you, leaving the big company and going on their own. They will speak to you about their ideas and ask for your comments. Usually they take what I believe is the wrong approach. They have, for example, thought of or developed and used a management process or method of training that they believe could become their 'product'. They have computerised it and think that with a bit of investment and work, that it could become marketable. And they could be right.

Unfortunately this gives them a product but not a product market. They do not have a product market until they have a customer. So this becomes my advice. Don't worry about products. There is a network of independent consultants out there who have a process or a training course, or a piece of software or whatever, to do anything a company might want to do, and, frankly, thousands of things companies will never want to do. And they will happily license you to sell it and deliver it, or will equally happily pay you 15% of the gross fees if you pass them a customer.

In other words, when you are thinking of going into consultancy concentrate on having a customer to work for immediately you are out and the product side will look after itself. Assume you can do anything with a bit of help from your colleagues, and work on the relationships with people in your current company or in your customers' or suppliers' companies. In this way, when the great day dawns, you can work out what they need and find through the network a method of satisfying that need.

It is quite easy to tag yourself into an appropriate network. Find out who are in similar skill areas to the ones you are going to bring to market, and talk to as many of them as possible. But for your selling work, concentrate first on bringing a market to a product, because that is the right way round.

Idea 21 – Start by booking your holidays

Very early on in my consultancy days I was with a client and took a booking to run a course. I wrote it in my diary. The same day Penny, my partner in the office, took a booking from another client for exactly the same days. She wrote it in the desk diary that I looked at from time to time. As luck would have it we discovered the double booking in time to avoid a difficult conversation with one of the clients, but we swore from then on to keep only one diary. Some people do this electronically but we have stayed with the same white board above the office desk. It is slightly embarrassing from time to time when I am at a meeting of the board of a client and the time comes for the next appointment to be booked. They take out their Psions and diaries or log on, while I have to excuse myself and make a phone call. 'Oh God, Ken's got to ask Penny if he is allowed to come', some say. But it is worth it for the security that we can never double book.

When you have got your consultancy going you will get repeat bookings. Customers will ring and offer you work on such and such a day. This is why it is so important to put red-letter days when you do not want to be working into your diary first of all. If you don't, you will find yourself not taking a break. I start each year by noting the first days of the two home test matches at Lords and the Oval. I then block out the weekends when I have to be at Murrayfield to watch the Scots humiliating various other nations at rugby. Next we put in the holidays. Only then do we start taking consultancy bookings.

Idea 22 – Don't let people smell fear

As a sales manager you quickly learn that success breeds success. If you have a salesperson well on target early on in the company year, you find that their selling and order-taking actually improves. They are exuding confidence and maybe saying to customers some things that they may have held back from if they were desperate for sales. It is a kind of controlled arrogance. 'Look do you want the product or not?'

The opposite shows itself when a salesperson is up against it. They are only on 20 per cent of target with only two months to go. They put pressure on their prospects; they surprise their customers with heavy-handed tactics and so on. Customers can smell fear and they don't like it.

So it is with consultancy. If you are sure that there is a market for your services, and you did the research (*didn't you?*), keep your confidence up and act happy. Play hard to get and do not be too available. Once you show anxiety and start, for example, to cut your daily rate, you are in trouble. *Courage, mon brave*, work hard, work smart but don't give off even a subtle tinge of fear.

Idea 23 – Go with the flow

The managing director of a chain of theme pubs told me 'A single creative act generates a stream of other creative acts.' Don't get too staid and fixed in the offerings you take to market. You will be surprised, when you have got going a bit, to find yourself going into situations that you did not envisage in your plan. As long as you know that you can offer a first-class service, take on some different things. Sometimes the flow can take you into new sources of revenues and new product markets.

Four Greatest Ideas for Working from the Office of Your Dreams

Introduction

For many people, working from home is a lifestyle thing. Gone are the rush-hour traffic jams and missed buses and trains. Instead you only have to wander through to the spare room – sorry, office – and you can always answer the office phone in your jim-jams if you decide to read the papers in bed or just have a lie-in that morning. But experienced home workers have found a few items of best practice to follow.

If, however, you decide you do need an actual office, you will find that it is in fact much cheaper in many ways to start up now. Telephone answering machines, coffee machines and ever-cheaper computing – enabling everyone to do their own typing – have greatly reduced the need for secretarial support. We are much more streamlined these days and this reduces the cost of premises.

But start with three ideas for working from home.

Idea 24 – Allocate enough space in the home

When my partner and I first set up business, we lived in a small flat with no spare room. Within six months not only could you hardly get into the sitting room for papers and files, but also the boots of both our cars were full of office stuff. It is extraordinary how much space you use up to run a business; so allocate yourself the maximum space you can consistent with the family still having a life, rather than the minimum you could manage with.

It is highly desirable to have a whole room for the business. Two main reasons – you are bound to expand, and you need to be able to shut the door on your office at the end of the day. Try not to let things spill over into the living area of the house. I know a couple who work from home each in a separate office. They place their working areas strictly out of bounds for their young children. When the baby-minder is there during the day, they actually communicate with each other by fax and e-mail to avoid going through the living area and being distracted by the children. They believe that home workers need to be even more expert at managing time than office workers, even perhaps to the extent of attending a time-management course.

They have strict rules about starting and finishing times. They ban weekend work and generally simulate a situation where their office could be in a different town, let alone building. When the kids are grown up you can be more selfish – one of the great advantages of working from home is you can do your work whenever you want. One of my colleagues, for example, works every Saturday morning and goes fishing during the week when the river banks are quieter.

When someone rings an office line they have a picture in their head of just that – an office. This is very useful and your way of working should not cancel this myth out unless you want it to.

Idea 25 – Find out what is tax-deductible

Treat your office as an office and charge the associated costs against your tax bill. I remember the VAT inspector querying the fact that we had bought a fridge and put it in the office storeroom. This seemed very unfair to us since there are very few offices of any size that do not have a fridge in them, and you can bet they were put against tax.

Allocate a fair proportion of cleaning repairs and redecorating to the business as well as a proportion of utilities bills and, of course, the telephone.

Idea 26 – Don't stint on telephone lines

When someone rings an office line they have a picture in their head of just that – an office. This is very useful and your way of working should not cancel this myth out unless you want it to. A consultant worked from a flat in London that he shared from time to time with his daughter. The managing director of one of his clients grew slightly suspicious of him when he phoned one day and was answered by the consultant's daughter accompanied by a loud crash. 'Sorry,' said the daughter, 'I dropped the iron.'

You cannot train children or teenagers to answer a telephone with anything except a loud 'Hallo?' so don't try. It is highly desirable to have three telephone lines. One is the number on your headed notepaper and cards. Keep this for incoming calls only so that people do not get the engaged tone too often. Use another line for outgoing calls and make that the one your children use.

It is a personal thing whether you use the call-waiting system where a caller trying to ring when the line is busy is told by a mechanical voice that they are trying to connect you. If you are not then connected, you know that the person you are trying to reach regards his or her current call as more important than yours. Besides which I can never remember how to use it, so the panic that ensues upsets the call you are already on as well as looking discourteous to the person trying to get through. We think it is better to get an answering machine and ban the kids from answering the office phone.

The third line is for the fax and Internet.

A final thought on working from home. Make sure that your family knows that you are going to work just as hard at home as you did when you went out to an office. They grew to accept the fact that you came home late quite often, but this a new situation. They may be surprised that you cannot join them when they are ready for tea, and so on. Pre-empt this because the nth time you hear the mumble, 'I don't know what you do up there all day', when you are sweating bricks to make a living can be quite irritating.

Idea 27 – Then get an office

Working from home implies a certain type of business – few people, if more than one, and very little capital put in at the start. If your business is going to be bigger than this, then make sure you have enough capital to get enough office space. One venture capital man I know believes wholeheartedly in hiring serviced office space. Even at £85 per square foot in London, he argued that the provision of reception, security, cleaning, and typing and photocopying by the sheet, made such an answer the ideal. This is so particularly because of the short term of the arrangement. If you grow more quickly than expected or, I suppose, if something goes wrong, you can get out of such a lease in a month. (Incidentally everyone I spoke to on the topic said that, however you do things, you should make sure you get more space than you need to begin with.)

'Look for grants from the Government and local authorities', said another. There are regional development grants that give you free space for, say, a year and some will give up to £50,000 as well. This led him to believe that it was foolish to put anything except a sales office in the south east of England or the Thames Valley. 'If you have, for example, a development department put them where there is less competition for the staff, and your office and their housing costs are much lower.'

Five Greatest Ideas for Financing Your Business

Introduction

If everyone had to finance their own businesses entirely, only the rich could even get started. Luckily, as well as your money – the share capital of the business – you can also get loan capital on a long- or short-term basis. So you need to think about some of the implications of this 'betting with someone else's money'. We will look at this again in the section on acquisitions. For the moment let's introduce two great ideas at the root of any business, cashflow, *Idea 28*, and leverage, *Idea 32*.

Idea 28 – Live by the two greatest financial mantras

Here are the watchwords of the realist, one from a banker and one from the director of finance of a local authority.

First greatest mantra: 'profit is an opinion, cash is reality'

A small builder has, say, two assets on his balance sheet, amongst others. One is a fixed asset of a cement mixer. It was purchased last year and the accountants agreed to its being written off over five years. The other is in his current assets and is some bags of cement. These are in stock and are valued at cost. His profits this year are reduced only by the depreciation on the fixed asset i.e. one-fifth of its price when bought. This could of course be very different from its value; indeed it is highly unlikely that second hand it will get nearly the residual value the balance sheet claims. The cement is not put against profits until it has been used in a contract and therefore sold. So in the opinion of the accountants and the owner of the business, these assets have little impact on this year's profits.

Now go and look at the yard where the assets are kept. It so happens that an apprentice emptied the cement into the mixer, added water, was called away to do something else and by an oversight left the cement in the mixer over the weekend. It solidified, as cement tends to do, rendering the stock of cement unusable and the mixer unfit for its purpose. What now should be the impact of these assets on this year's profit and loss account? We know, and so does the builder, that the value on the balance sheet should be written off now, knocking a significant sum of money off the bottom line. But, we happen also to know, this would not please the bank manager one little bit. He or she was promised profits at such and such a level and that is what they want to see. So the builder wheels the mixer into a dark corner of the yard and everyone is happy. Profit is an opinion.

Reality strikes only when the builder needs cement and a mixer; it will cost cash to hire a mixer and buy the raw materials. So cash is reality.

Second greatest mantra: 'in a cost benefit analysis, the costs are absolutely real, the benefits are a sort of dream.'

The art of running the business of your dreams includes making assessments of the future. The only certainty about such assessments is that they will be wrong. But you are much more likely to overestimate the income stream or profits, than overestimate the costs. Suppose you have to hire good people and pay them high salaries, that is a fair business risk. But it is good practice to look at the return you will get on them very gloomily and then half it. That is probably the only certain way to avoid disappointment. Give people time in your plan to come up to speed in terms of the contribution you have hired them for.

A guru once did a planning session for a couple of guys who wanted to run a pub as a sideline. They did their business plan and asked for his opinion. The profitability and cashflow was pretty good. 'What would happen,' said the sage 'if the sales turnover were half of that?' They went away adjusted the costs and came back proving that they could still break even or make a slight profit if sales were halved. 'Now halve it again', advised the guru. 'What!' said one of them, 'If we want to break even at that level of sales we would have to empty the ashtrays ourselves.' 'Exactly,' said the guru. They emptied the ashtrays for three months while the business got up to speed and delivered the business plan.

So concentrate on your cashflow and be realistic to pessimistic about income and returns. Incidentally, some people duck the issue of overestimating sales simply by never writing down a forecast. That doesn't work either.

Idea 29 – What kind of trader are you?

Try not to spend too much time worrying over the status of the trading company you are setting up. Normally it is pretty straightforward. If, for example, you are going to put a lot of capital in and hire a load of people you will want to be a limited company. Otherwise you will want to be a sole trader or partnership. You have to check the tax situation – see *don't economise on tax advice Idea 93–* and decide accordingly. A partnership can be very tax efficient if you are setting up a business that involves your partner in life. A partnership also gives you the opportunity to raise money by bringing in another partner who puts in capital to buy himself or herself in.

If you are a sole trader, just about your only source of funds is your banker or possibly your friends and family.

The choice for raising funds is much wider if you are a limited company, but there is more paperwork and expense involved in keeping up with the red tape.

Setting up as a sole trader

- Tell your local tax inspector and contributions agency. You may be surprised how helpful these people are, and they have loads of brochures that cover most situations.
- Make sure there is no planning problem with starting a business in the location you have chosen.
- If you give your business a different name from your own, don't forget to include your name somewhere on your headed notepaper.
- Decide, probably by talking to the VAT office, whether or not you need to register for VAT.

Setting up as a partnership:

The only drawback of a partnership is that each partner is jointly liable for the debts of the partnership. This means that if there is trouble, no matter who caused it, your assets, including your home if you own it, are at risk. This means that the degree of trust required in a partnership is very high indeed. Except with your life partner, and even some would say in that case, never have an informal partnership arrangement. It is relatively easy to get a general partnership agreement that could fit your case; otherwise you may have to explain what you want to a lawyer and pay for a tailored agreement.

Think ahead and make sure that the agreement covers any eventuality. Make sure the agreement describes in detail how the business will be managed and controlled. Keep in mind the next idea.

Setting up a limited company

Get a starter pack from Companies House. The easiest way to set up a limited company is to buy one off the shelf from a company formation specialist. To set up a private limited company you need one director and a company secretary who cannot be the sole director. You can start such a company with very little capital indeed. The starter pack tells you what forms and fees to send.

You may want to set up a public limited company. PLC can look more substantial and impressive than Ltd although there is little difference. A PLC must have an authorised share capital of £50,000 and a quarter of that must be issued. In other words you must put in at least £12,500 to get started.

When you are setting up a company, the important issue is to get started producing and selling your products and services. For this reason it is likely that you will benefit from using an accountant who will take you through the processes and tell you, for example, what meetings to convene and what resolutions to pass.

Idea 30 – Don't assume that fraud cannot happen to you

In the experience of the people I have talked to, and in my own experience, fraud is rare. Most people live reasonably honest lives. This means that if fraud does impact you it is all the more surprising and dispiriting.

(A good friend of mine some years ago had a brother who committed fraud, and who was destined for prison unless his friends and family paid off the people he had defrauded. We all chipped in against his promise to repay us in five years. Since neither he nor I had any idea where we would be in five years, we arranged to meet at Piccadilly Circus on the 1 January 1980. To his credit he pitched up that day and paid me back.)

An accountant I know got into bad trouble as the result of a partner fiddling the books in his partnership. The son of one of the key people of a cleaning firm was put in charge of the mailroom. He made money on the side by systematically changing the values on invoices and pocketing the difference. Actually, this practice did not last long since he omitted to alter the VAT total pro rata. So, it can happen. Guard against it and insure against it if necessary. The key is at the planning stage of anything to put in such safeguards as seem like a sledgehammer to crack a nut, but that might be in five years' time a very necessary procedure.

We have 20 people in our investment club. We wrote the original rules with, for example, four people, one of whom is not the treasurer, required to sign a cheque of any size. 'Anyone would think that there was hundreds of thousands of pounds at stake here', grumbled one member who thought we were overdoing it when the fund scarcely exceeded two thousand pounds. He does not grumble now when the fund is worth a quarter of a million.

Be sensible – trust people but get the security of formal agreements round you at all times.

The easiest way to borrow money for a new business is to agree that the owner's houses should be mortgaged against the loan. You should resist this at all costs.

Idea 31 – Don't bet the house

The easiest way to borrow money for a new business is to agree that the owner's houses should be mortgaged against the loan. You should resist this at all costs. If your business does not make it, it will be a nasty time to be homeless. If it all goes wrong at least you could sell or let your house until you got yourself fixed up with another source of income. It can be done. Use your track record as a businessperson to persuade lenders that you are likely to make the dream come true. Make the dream look achievable and not pie in the sky. Speak to more than one potential lender, play one off against another and negotiate a different kind of guarantee.

Be careful, banks will sometimes only ask for a personal guarantee rather than a mortgage on your house. If you own your house it has the same effect.

Idea 32 – Give me but one firm spot on which to stand …

This quote from Archimedes continues, 'and I will move the world.' He is referring to the phenomenon of leverage and claiming that with a long enough lever and somewhere to stand he could literally reposition the world. There are two main aspects of leverage that lend themselves to building the business of your dreams – financial leverage and operating leverage.

Most people have at least one 'leveraged play' in their financial life. They buy a house using a little of their own money and a lot of the building society's. If the asset increases in value, as it always has done over the long term, then the profits gained go only to the borrower, who only has to carry out the obligation to the building society of paying the interest and repaying the capital. This can have an extraordinary impact on your finances. Suppose you buy a house for £100,000 using £10,000 of your own money and borrowing £90,000. Twenty-five years later even if you have not paid off the loan the asset has become worth, say, £250,000. This £160,000 is all yours giving an average return on your original £10,000 investment of £6400 or more than 60% per annum. It is almost impossible, except with a really long-odds bet like the lottery, to do better than that. (Incidentally if a pedant says that I should reduce the return by the cost of the loan interest I reply that you had to live somewhere and the interest was the cost of having somewhere to live.)

The point is that you are making return on someone else's money. So it is in business.

If you put in £10,000 and a bank puts in £90,000 to buy a business valued at £100,000, then if you double the profits and therefore the value of the business you get the return of £100,000 for your initial outlay of £10,000. If you have doubled the profits in a year or two, that return is pretty good.

This is, of course, another reason for not giving ownership of the business away in share options and so forth when the value is low. Anyway, so much for financial leverage; now let's look at its cousin, operating leverage.

There is a huge benefit to be gained if a division or a company can increase its sales volumes without increasing its fixed costs. It illustrates what managers are often talking about. 'We have to sweat the assets.' When you have spent money on infrastructure of any sort, slight increases in sales have an unexpectedly high impact on the bottom line.

The concept of operating leverage shows the benefit of this.

Look at the impact on the bottom line of different splits between variable and fixed costs. Each of the four profit and loss accounts is built to answer the same question. 'If we can increase sales volume by 10% without increasing fixed costs what percentage impact will it have on net profit?' Operating leverage is calculated by dividing this percentage by 10%.

First case

	£ current	£ additional 10%
sales	100	110
variable costs	90	99
contribution	10	11
fixed costs	0	0
net profit	10	11 (an increase of 10%)

The operating leverage is 1, i.e. there is no leverage at all.

Second case

	£ current	£ additional 10%
sales	100	110
variable costs	60	66
contribution	40	44
fixed costs	30	30
net profit	10	14 (an increase of 40%)

The operating leverage is 4.

Third case

	£ current	£ additional 10%
sales	100	110
variable costs	30	33
contribution	70	77
fixed costs	60	60
net profit	10	17 (an increase of 70%)

The operating leverage is 7.

Fourth case

	£ current	£ additional 10%
sales	100	110
variable costs	0	0
contribution	100	110
fixed costs	90	90
net profit	10	20 (an increase of 100%)

The operating leverage is 10.

I cannot leave leverage without mentioning the potential downside even although it hardly fits into the business of your dreams. The upside potential of leverage is matched by the downside risk. If you have operating leverage of 5, then a 10% improvement in your sales will produce a 50% improvement in you profits. A 10% drop in sales will produce 5 times that decrease in profits. If you have financial leverage the down side is as dramatic as the benefit.

Nevertheless, a great tip for building the business of your dreams is: bet with someone else's money.

Four Greatest Ideas for Staffing Your Business

Introduction

In any business, and particularly those where the staff are the company's main assets, hiring the right people is crucial. You can get lots of help in this but it is expensive, *Idea 33*. There is risk and return here as usual. Talented people are more difficult to manage than drones, so make sure you hire people appropriate for your Dreams and objectives, Idea 34. Here are some *do*s and *don't*s born of solid and sometimes very painful experience.

Idea 33 – Grow your own head-hunters

Using head-hunters is a luxury that a new business, and any business that you happen to own, should avoid. Put simply they have two major flaws:

- They are very expensive. Not only that, but if you take the advice of this book and negotiate for everything, it may not work with these particular people. Suppose you negotiate their commission down from 25% of first year salary of the person they place to say 15%, which is entirely possible; you end up with the awful feeling that you may not be getting a look at the best potential staff members because they are reserved for the people who pay full whack.
- By definition you do not have any first-hand knowledge of the candidates nor even reliable second-hand knowledge of the individual derived from a person who is 100% on your side.

There are three key elements to hiring someone. Do you trust them? Can you and your team work with them? Are they competent or better than competent at the job? Most experienced businesspeople would put the questions in that order of significance. The role of the head-hunter can now be seen to be operating on the least important of these three questions. They should be reliable on whether candidates have the skills and experience to do the proposed job, but have less knowledge of whether the new business can trust them or work with them.

To be sure you can trust someone really needs good previous knowledge of him or her. Hire from people you knew in your last company or from your customers and suppliers. Hire from any source if you know the person you are going to hire, if you trust him or her and if you are convinced you can work with them, probably because you have worked with them in the past.

Second best to this is to hire people who are known to those you already trust and work with – that is your existing staff. If you do not use head-hunters you can afford to be very generous in offering incentives for your staff to introduce new people from their acquaintances and colleagues. Do this and lo and behold you have grown your own head-hunters.

Idea 34 – Hire the people who fit your dream

Leadership is the skill of persuading people to co-operate willingly to achieve results. Managing people is a mixture of motivation and manipulation. So far so good. Unfortunately there is often a correlation between people who are talented and well able to help you take your business forward, and people who are difficult to control. After all, by definition you would not work for them; so don't expect them to take working for you as necessarily their end game. But if you need such people take them on but keep in mind the need to stay in control.

Be careful of the syndrome where you hire a number two and they bring in from their previous employment number three, and then number four, and so on. You must avoid any possibility of their forming an internal Mafia that could threaten to form a cabal and threaten your control.

If the main purpose of a person's work is to sell your products and services, then hire salespeople. They will want an incentive scheme and will drive a coach and horses through any errors you make in drawing up the scheme, but good ones are indeed the main engine for the growth of the business. You should not have to debate giving them shares in the business – their skill is in selling not necessarily in managing anything. One entrepreneur said to me, 'Hire salespeople and expect them to earn out and burn out. No small business needs an old salesperson.' He appeared somewhat dismissive of the sales type despite their crucial importance in chasing sales growth. But at least you can get them without giving them bits of the company.

So, you want to be a leader? Make your mind up what sort of person you want to lead.

Other people with production or development skills are likely to need different incentives. They will certainly, once they have realised their importance to the business, want a share in the equity of the business. It is a difficult decision. Most owners are understandably reluctant to give shares away even as options to be earned. Generally they avoid it unless it is absolutely necessary – like if the person might go into competition with you. If you do give shares away, get a good price for them in money or in effort and achievement and don't lose control. Whilst we can agree 80% of something is worth more than 100% of nothing, that is a business you cannot sell, we can also agree that it is your dream; so try not to give more than that proportion away.

If you are building a lifestyle business, the last thing you want is troublesome staff. So hire for their ability to more or less cover for you and carry out a function, but don't expect them to come up with any whiz-kid ideas, or serve the customers as well as you do.

Finally, whatever type of objective you have in mind, remember that the most important asset any business has, particularly any small business, is its relationships with the main customers, some suppliers and the bank. Never delegate these. By all means let other people run everything and enjoy life; but keep close tabs on these relationships. (If you get into trouble, it is more likely to be an amenable customer than an amenable bank manager who will get you back on course.)

So, you want to be a leader? Make your mind up what sort of person you want to lead.

Idea 35 – Ask the customer

The key to a good hire is the acceptability of the person's experience, knowledge and even personality to your key customers. This is mainly true, of course, if the person you are hiring will have direct contact with these people, but is also true for back-room people who will have an influence on either your product or your terms for doing business. So, before you hire anyone, introduce them to at least one of your key customers. The feedback is invaluable.

Keep the meeting very low key and make sure that the customer is aware that they are being asked for an opinion not being asked to make your decision. Just arrange for you and the candidates individually to meet the customer for a short time. Make sure that you leave them on their own for a while. After this, your customer's view will confirm or deny your feelings about the person – very useful.

There are two main advantages of this approach. Firstly your customer will be pleased with the trouble you are taking and, secondly, you will get an authoritative view on the industry knowledge and customer awareness of the candidate. There is a downside. If the customer does not like the person and you still hire them, you will have to put extra effort into starting the relationship between the two. And the opposite is also true; if you decide not to go ahead with a candidate that the customer recommended, you risk some disappointment.

But in the experience of a lot of people, the advantages vastly outweigh the disadvantages. This is true when you think about the enormous problem of getting rid of staff you do not need or are not performing. If your customer can help to avoid even one of those, you have proved the usefulness of this idea.

Idea 36 – Keep people in your variable costs

Firing poor performers is an expensive business, as is letting people go because you do not have the level of work for them that you were expecting. And do not underestimate the negative affect that this will have on morale. There is much less employee loyalty around now than was the case, mainly due to the behaviour of employers who, in reacting to very fast changes in the business environment, have themselves being showing markedly less loyalty in the other direction. This means that people are more than willing to move to a competitor to build their careers.

So, if you make wrong decisions in staffing and have to put them right, you may find yourself with a morale problem leading to the loss of the people you desperately needed to keep.

One way out of this dilemma of 'Do we need another person and is this the right one,' is to use temps and contractors. (Be very careful of the tax position on contractors, especially in the IT business. The government is bearing down on contractors who use their employer's equipment and have only one customer. They regard such individuals as being in reality employees and want the tax and National Insurance contributions appropriate to that status.)

But temps and contractors are not in fixed costs. You can dispense with their services whenever you want and they are never regarded as full members of the team. This means that their departure is met with more equanimity than if they were. The two disadvantages of this approach are cost and the fact that you have no hold over the people either. But remember leverage, *Idea 32* – the more you have in variable costs, the more efficient use you make of fixed costs.

Four Greatest Ideas for Keeping In Touch with Your Market

Introduction

The customer is king. Have I mentioned that before? The customer is also changing his or her mind about what they want regularly. You have to exploit this, and protect yourself from the downside of change, by expanding your market, *Idea 37*, continuously. And it is not just you that needs to keep in touch, don't forget the other people in the organisation, *Idea 39*. These are four ideas that do not require a lot of effort except perhaps *Idea 38*, where we look at the knotty problem of keeping your customers in touch with you, and looking the part even when you lack substance in reality.

Idea 37 – Prospect continuously

A hole in the order book now is a hole in the cashflow in about two months' time.

We all have a background from one part of business before we start on the business of our dreams. We come from production, sales, finance or wherever and this dictates some of the emphasis that we put into the business. One of the advantages of coming with a sales background is a complete understanding of the disciplines of prospecting.

Salespeople also know that when you are selling you are not delivering and earning revenue, and when you are delivering and earning revenue you are not selling. It is easy to let your business life reflect this in a cycle – easy, but dangerous. A hole in the order book now is a hole in the cashflow, *Idea 55*, in about two months' time. This delay can give you a false sense of security especially when you are busy delivering and find it hard to fit in what needs to be done in that part of the business let alone add selling time. But that is what you must do.

Set aside an hour each week for prospecting – finding new clients – or more if your business demands it. During this hour make your phone calls or send out your mailshots or devise your new brilliant gimmicks for generating potential customers. Never, ever miss it out. I always do it on a Monday morning since that tends to be the time that other salespeople are in their weekly meetings or touching base with their offices or whatever.

Don't waste prospecting effort. If you send out a mailshot and you are in a business where you need to follow up with a phone call, i.e. most businesses, don't send a huge number out at the same time. Send out enough that you have sufficient numbers to ring to fulfil your prospecting quota. This drip-feed technique has the added advantage that you have to go back to it on a regular basis, thus automatically putting the hour-a-week discipline in place.

Idea 38 – Size does count

Small companies face the challenge all the time of trying to look bigger than they are. You will use all the normal devices:

- Hold all your meetings on your customers' premises. It's terrific; you drink their coffee and possibly get lunch as well.
- If they are coming to your location, arrange to be at a hotel either in the lobby or in the restaurant
- Use phone forwarding so that you keep in touch. I find it quite witty to be talking to a customer who has phoned a Berkshire number while actually I am cooling my tootsies in a swimming pool in Spain.
- Don't stint on letterhead and design on the documents you send out. The John Bull printing press look screams 'sole trader'.

• Publish a newsletter or refer your customers and prospects to one on a Web page. It takes time and you have to work hard at it so that it does not become actually or perceptively out of date. People tend not to read a company description on a Website that has not been updated for a year or more.

Idea 39 – Get everyone to talk to customers regularly

The way to keep every member of your staff in touch with reality is to allow very few of them to be completely unexposed to customers. You can do this individually by insisting that your product developer attends customer progress meetings, for example, or *en masse* by inviting the customer to come and speak at the annual company get together. I have seen engineers, for example, completely transform the way they think about their work when they are given a real insight into what the customers are trying to do, and how they look at your offerings.

Do you know how to get very expensive advertising space free of charge? Easy – when you, or anyone of yours, are meeting someone at an airport always display a professional placard with the name of your company on it. Do it even if you are meeting your mother. If you do this for 20 minutes at Heathrow, for example, some 300 influential business people will have read your company name.

Idea 40 – Speak to the press

The trade press, and indeed the national press, are always looking for stories. They have a lot of white space to fill regularly. Feed them what you can. Study the trade press and get to know the journalists. Eventually they will start to ask you for comments on stories they have got from an alternative source. This gives you a profile outside your organisation and is good for improving your 'gravitas'. To my knowledge, and astonishment, a mention in the British Airways in-flight magazine is read by a lot of people that you want to impress; and they are impressed just by reading a name they know – yours or your company's.

Seven Greatest Ideas for Helping a Business Customer to Buy Wisely

Introduction

This section and the next are about business-to-business selling. It has been interesting how the innovators on the Internet have built valuable business propositions in the first place by looking at its possibilities in terms of business-to-consumer. The advantage of such an approach is, of course, that the numerical size of the potential market is so huge, that any business that secures a fraction of it and sells at a profit is going to look as though future potential profits are huge. (A favourite maxim of mine states, 'a small percentage of a large number is a large number.' This is very helpful when you are trying to sell a business idea or a method of improving productivity.) But, as a gross generalisation, margins in business-to-business trading tend to be better than in its consumer equivalent. Also, although the competitive risk can be high, business-to-business trading tends to give you bigger jumps in growth. If you pull off the big deal to BT or sell a small services contract to the BBC, you may be on the way to rapid expansion. Indeed, looking at the new Internet applications providers now gives a different picture where business-to-business has a higher profile. The set-up costs are probably higher and the time to prepare to trade longer. This means that the capital required at the start is also bigger; but the credibility of signing on actual business customers gives a more solid look to the Internet wannabees.

A favourite maxim of mine states, 'a small percentage of a large number is a large number.' This is very helpful when you are trying to sell a business idea or a method of improving productivity.

Having IBM as a signed-up user is worth an awful lot of prospect databases. So, what is the key to building the business-to-business of your dreams whether Internet-based or not? Well, start from knowing your customers' business as well as they know it themselves, and see everything including your sales campaign from the customers' point of view. If you can help them make a sensible business decision based on business logic, you are well on the way to becoming a trusted and preferred supplier. So this section covers the buying cycle and the next selling cycle.

Idea 41 – Encourage sensible buying decisions

The concept of 'knowing a customer's business better than they do' neatly encapsulates the concept of helping a customer to go about decision-making in a logical manner. There is a huge amount of emotion in any significant buying decision, and we will have to build that into the plan, but it is best to have the emotion sitting on a rock of good common sense.

Let us take as an example a company making a capital investment decision. This could be an IT hardware and software project, new turbines for a power station or any other investment that is going to give service and add value for a protracted length of time. How do you go about buying such a solution?

A *sensible* company's guide to capital investment

At any point in time a company is being offered by its managers and by outsiders many more ideas than it can afford to implement. There is constant pressure for money from product-development managers, designers, information technology groups and others throughout the business. This causes most companies to develop management processes for investment appraisal and project management.

To understand this process, we need to follow the *sensible* company's step-by-step guide to capital investment appraisal and implementation.

Step 1 – Establish the objectives of the project within the company's business strategy

Many projects have as their starting point a strategic objective of the company. Indeed, if you look at the way banks have implemented their IT systems, you will find that they have followed the rule of maintaining competitiveness by keeping abreast of new technology developments. From the seller's point of view this 'me too' strategy is a fortuitous starting point.

It is likely, however, that an overall strategic reason for buying will not be sufficient on its own, and managers will have to back it up with a solid tactical or business case. It is also important that investment projects support the other key business strategies such as product or marketing strategies. This is the first hurdle over which any proposal must jump. In other words, you must connect the benefits of the products you are selling to these high-level policies. Notice how already we have moved to the customer's point of view. A benefit is only a benefit if the customer has agreed it to be so.

Step 2 – Involve the management and staff who will have their jobs changed as a result of the project

The only certainty about any capital investment is that the jobs of some people are going to change. Most large organisations are getting better at managing such change. There are, however, still some, along with many smaller businesses, who handle this part of the process at best insufficiently and at worst with a lack of sensitivity. This imperils the success of the project.

Do not confuse this stage with training. It is helping the people involved to understand the benefits of change to their company, their customers and themselves. Sometimes managers deliberately keep the approaching change secret from staff, only to be mugged by them when the change has to be implemented. I worked with another manager to try to convince a power station manager to tell the unions, as early as possible in the buying cycle, about a new system that would involve them all. We failed, and the strike lasted for three weeks and the settlement cost a fortune.

If a company you are selling to ignores this familiarisation stage in the implementation plan, you can gain competitive edge by helping the customer recognise the need for early warning systems.

Step 3 – Agree the tactical business case including the cost justification

In almost all companies there is a standard method of making a business case and it is vital that people who are going to sell capital goods to them know what that process is. How close the customer allows you to that process depends on your relationship, and how much value the customer believes you can add to the process. If you know the value of the project to the customer, you are obviously in a much stronger position when it comes to negotiating the price.

Step 4 – Establish implementation priorities and controls

During this step in the buying process, the sensible customer puts in the basics of project management. It is crucial at this stage to see the project in its entirety and plan the milestones which allow the business and technical mangers to control the implementation.

The key is to document every action and ensure that all the milestones have easy measurement. It is not enough to state, 'Test system for user acceptance.' The salesperson and customer together must describe the tests in detail and agree the measures of user acceptance.

The job of you the seller in this phase of the project plan is to suggest all the activities involved to ensure a successful implementation. Very frequently there are issues the supplier is aware of which may be unknown to the customer.

From previous experience, the supplier can anticipate some pitfalls and problems, and avoid unnecessary surprises. It can be tempting to duck some of these issues and leave customers unaware of something they will probably have to face and solve in the fullness of time. Once again competitive edge is available here. Your pointing out an additional factor unplanned by the potential customer can damage the credibility of your competitor.

It is not possible to overstate the importance of getting this phase right and assisting the prospect to plan the project from the start, right through to successful completion. You can use an assumptive close in working with the prospect on the outline implementation plan by including the placing of the order in the project plan.

Step 5 – Select the exact functionality

This is the part of the project plan that the technical enthusiasts in the customer tend to enjoy. They survey the market for new technologies, study other implementations and talk to lots of suppliers. From these ideas they produce the detailed functionality.

Salespeople are also well aware of the work done at this time. They have two concerns: using time wisely and meeting the customer specification.

Firstly, is the customer using your time wisely or are you wasting valuable selling time? Avoid the pitfall of two technicians, one the salesperson and the other the customer, spending lots of time looking at all the options now and in the future. It's all very well demonstrating all the possibilities, but if the customer has no commitment to doing something at all levels of management who will be involved in the decision, then you are better off elsewhere. I have seen salespeople spend ages with an enthusiast only to find that the decision makers of whether the project happened or not were miles up the organisation.

The second point of concern for salespeople at this stage is to make sure that their products and services can do what the customer requires. From an understanding of their offerings and of the competitions', they will try to ensure that any unique elements in their portfolio have a place in the customer requirement.

The end of this stage is the production of a document outlining the exact specification of the technology the prospect wants to buy. You must get involved in this. You will be at a significant disadvantage during the tendering process if your competition is helping the customer write the specification.

I well remember in times gone by, a British manufacturer spelt the word for computer storage 'disc', while their main American competitor spelt it 'disk'. Sales people were always eager to see which spelling the prospect chose in the tender document, as this was an indication of where their preference lay.

Step 6 – Select the necessary products and services and their suppliers

Senior management has a number of concerns. The key issue for them is that their managers choose the correct suppliers. This ensures that the project is successful, measured by 'on time and within budget'. They want the best deal possible, sometimes measured by 'the cheapest', but in complex projects frequently described as 'best value for money'.

Another issue is that their managers subject the project to their normal tendering procedures. They want to be sure that no-one brings unreasonable pressure on their technicians or buyers which would lead to them selecting a particular supplier and making a mistake.

The board looks at any capital investment project in terms of its relevance to the business and to its main strategies. 'Is it hitting at the key issues we are facing and assisting with the implementation of our key strategies?' 'Is it part of our general direction and will it remain so for the life of the project?'

Then the board worries about organisational change. 'Does the project demand difficult or uncomfortable changes in organisation?' 'Will the project still be relevant and feasible after we have made other planned changes?' This last issue is made more significant if the buyers and implementation managers of the project are unaware of the impending change. It's like bank technicians improving the back office system while the directors are planning to close all the branches.

So, the end of the buying phase comes, you have seen it from the customer's point of view and, hey presto, you've got your order. Well done.

Idea 42 – Deliver products on time and within budget

At this point in the process the customer is ready to take delivery of the products and services he or she has ordered. All they want is for what was proposed to become what actually happens. So we will look at this part of the buying process only from the seller's point of view.

If building a business involves building satisfactory relationships with customers, then one of the best ways, not to say most obvious, of doing this is simply to keep your promises. Put someone in charge of that and make it quite clear to the customer who that someone is. That person then has the overriding concern of ensuring that the supplying company achieves its commitments. He or she will ensure that it meets all its deadlines and produces complete customer satisfaction by living up to expectations. People often say, and it is certainly true, that the job of such a delivery manager is as much about selling internally as to customers. When companies make complex proposals, particularly ones that involve new products or services, there is always a risk that something will go wrong.

It is also frequently true that, during the sales campaign, you will have stretched your company to the full to make sure that the offering is competitive. This stretching process adds to the risk and it requires some dedication to keep your company up to the mark.

You may have dreadful conflicts of priorities at this time. When you are involved in delivering or implementing, you are not involved in selling. In a small business this leads to peaks and troughs of orders and deliveries with the subsequent cashflow problems. But then, if you keep selling and don't deliver, you will eventually come unstuck anyway. The goal is to do business with the customer frequently and for ever. It is a waste of time to try to develop a customer if there is any suggestion of dissatisfaction. You have to see the effort involved as building for future orders as well as delivering today's.

Make sure that the person taking responsibility for delivery does not form so cosy a relationship with the customer that they become an oasis of competence, at least in their view, in a desert of your business's cackhandedness. I have often seen project managers with good relationships with their customers fall into the trap of blaming their people or their company for any shortfalls in performance and not taking accountability themselves.

This is a short-term attitude and in the extreme leads to a situation where the customer puts his arm round your shoulder, if you are such a project manager, and explains that while he has no problem with you, the supplying organisation is not up to it and he is going elsewhere.

Idea 43 – Take lost business very seriously

From time to time you or your people will drop the ball. If this causes you to lose a customer, take it very seriously. Ask politely but firmly for a meeting with the most senior person on the customer's side who had some involvement with the decision. You may have to write a letter to make this happen, since a telephone call can make you sound aggressive. Make sure the letter accepts the decision that has been made. Don't look as though you are trying to reopen the sales campaign.

At the meeting itself try not to go defensive or argumentative. Remember, the customer has made the right decision. They are convinced of that so you may as well believe it. Actually that is not strong enough, you should believe it because it damn well is true.

The best way of ensuring the right approach is to use their terms. 'What was your basis of decision?', and 'On which points did we fall down?' will get you the information you require. Be prepared to discover customer criteria that you were unaware of during the sales campaign or during the period when you were delivering product. Criteria do change, and the original decision to buy from you may have been made on grounds totally different from the current way that the customer looks at alternatives. Try to get the person to talk about your people, but do it sensitively. You do not want to have to agree implicitly with a criticism that may make it difficult to propose that that person works with the customer again.

The test of whether you have understood from the customer's point of view what went wrong is if you are able to do a good summary of it at the end of the meeting and subsequently in writing.

So, you have finished finding out why you are on a lost business visit, and you have learned the lessons it offers, it is now time to put the boot in. I know I *said* that you should suggest to the senior person that you were going to reopen the campaign, and that probably remains good advice for most of the meeting. But towards the end you must have some way of offering to do something or to accept a consolation order or anything that will enable you and your company to stay in touch with the customer. Remember it is always easier to build on existing customers rather than finding new ones, so always try to get back in except, I suppose, where things have gone so wrong that there is no way that the customer will give you a fair crack of the whip. In this last case, thank the person and retire 'bloody but unbowed.'

Idea 44 – Make sure your business processes deliver

Look at the customer facing processes you are building separately from all the others. I know that all business processes eventually lead to the customer, but the direct interface ones are the ones that can get you into trouble. It is very important for the responsible manager to be present at significant moments in the life of an investment project. Professional salespeople make it a practice, for example, to be there when significant deliveries of products occur.

I was once involved in the delivery of a large computer to an old Victorian building. The only method of getting the machine in was to remove a part of the roof and lower the machine in by crane. The mobile crane had a journey of some 100 miles to get to the building. I had not done business with the crane company before and we had put a lot of effort into ensuring that it was there on time and did not let us down.

When it came to the day, the crane arrived absolutely on the dot and the engineers and others who were there for the installation were in their appointed places. The customer's IT director had come to watch the event as had I, the account manager. The only thing that failed to make it was the computer itself, which had unaccountably rescheduled itself for delivery the following day.

The embarrassment of sending the crane back along with the engineers and, of course, the IT director was bad enough. The only mitigating factor was that I was there to handle the feelings of the customer, reorganise all the activities and prepare for the actual delivery date. It was a very uncomfortable moment made slightly better by the knowledge that my absence would have resulted in an even worse situation.

Idea 45 – Who needs training? Your customer needs training

If you are selling complex products and services, the customer needs your training services to make sure that they can use the product, get the most out of it, without using an inordinate amount of your support people's time in follow-up work and become satisfied customers. Selling such training services may not be simple. You are, of course, selling your products and services as being easy to use, right? 'Well, if they are easy to use, why do I need training as well?' says your customer. But it does not much matter what type of business you are in; ask yourself 'What ideally would the customer pay for in terms of training?' Then plan to offer just that. The point is that customer satisfaction depends on their ability to achieve the benefits they are expecting. Look at it as an chance to sell services and, if you have your people involved in doing the training, for the courses to give the delegates good feelings, build your reputation and give you feedback on future repeat opportunities.

So, try to ensure that your customer does not take any short cuts in what can be a crucial phase in a complex project. The lack of adequate training can be a major source of customer dissatisfaction.

Idea 46 – Gain a reputation as a solution seller

Finally in this business-to-business selling section, let us draw some conclusions. A good job title for the person doing solution selling or looking after a major customer is 'account manager'. The account manager may be the managing director in point of fact, but it is in the role of account manager that they will benefit from the *sensible* customer's guide to capital investment

If the account manager is to be truly customer facing, he or she will be with the customer as he undertakes each stage in the process. That could be the definition of the difference between being a solution seller or just a seller.

A seller will become involved with the project only when invited by the prospect at the step 'select functionality' or even worse at the step 'select the necessary products and services and the suppliers of them.' This leads to bickering about the features of you product against theirs.

The solution seller will involve himself from start to finish and may even instigate the whole idea by being the first person to identify the opportunity. This is easier to write down and say than it is to do, since there are hazards to this sort of consultative selling:

- The customer may want to keep aspects of the project, e.g. return on investment, to himself.
- The customer may not see the requirement for carrying out each of the steps.
- It is time consuming.
- It requires the account manager to become versed in his or her customer's business and hold discussions on business topics which initially may not be part of a salesperson's comfort zone.
- The approach carries some risk, in that a customer going methodically through a process of this nature may come across reasons for not doing the project as well as reasons for doing it.

With all these hazards it is still the essence of professional account management to try to persuade a customer to identify the steps in capital investment evaluation and then go through them together. So, amend this step-by-step guide to fit the products and services that you sell. You might also benefit from taking a project whose implementation is complete and trying, as a post-hoc rationalisation, to recognise what happened at each step. You can then take the result to the customer concerned, discuss it with them and try to sell them on the idea of involving you in the next project they are planning.

As you do this, use your experience and your company's to prove that you can add value to your customer's professional plans.

Idea 47 – Look back in wonder

The final step in the customer's sensible progress through the capital investment process is to evaluate the results and adapt the project to improve them.

The sensible customer will take this issue very seriously. In most cases the technicians delivering something new will liaise with the users to find out whether they are getting what they want. They will also agree the necessary improvements.

This iteration takes them back to the phase of the project 'select functionality'. This type of evaluation is important but the customer should not stop there. Equally important is checking that the project is producing the benefits agreed at the step that established the business case. There is a prevalent attitude saying 'We have spent the money and we are not going to go back to the old way, so why bother checking the return on investment?'

There are dangers in this attitude. If managers believe that no audit will take place, they will tend to produce business cases which are much more optimistic than they would otherwise be. Similarly the skills in producing business cases will not develop unless management monitors the results of each project.

Take a computer example. A number of large companies and government institutions have developed large centralised systems. They have then obliged their user community to use them as generalised systems. Finally they have tinkered with the functionality and failed to take a long cold look at the benefits and relevance of their centralised processes.

This has led to inappropriate systems and user dissatisfaction, sometimes on a very big scale. Resolving this situation is very costly but, if not undertaken, will almost certainly cost the organisations the loss of competitive edge.

A further reason why the account manager wants to assist the customer to audit cost justification is the need for reference sites. These are much more convincing if they can demonstrate business benefits as well as technical achievement.

This checking mechanism takes the customer back to the business case. The other check is of course on the strategic relevance of the project. The customer needs to ask the questions, 'Is this still relevant?', and 'Could we make changes to improve the project's contribution to the overall direction of the business?'

Positive answers to all of this will give the supplier of the last project much more chance of becoming the supplier of the next one as well.

Six Greatest Ideas for Selling Big Ticket Items – Business to Business

Introduction

If you sell complex products to business, there is a right and a wrong way of going about it. Or, rather, there are some processes, evolved over time by professional salespeople, to help you on your way. These processes form the ideas in this section. After all you cannot build the business of your dreams without taking orders. So learn professional selling by following the techniques in *Ideas 52* and *53*. First let's check on the definition of 'big ticket selling.'

Idea 48 – Sell a solution to a problem or an opportunity

I once worked with a team who were planning a sales campaign to persuade a major telecommunications company to buy public exchanges (or switches) from their company rather than from any of a group of competitors. The planning team was, needless to say, very senior in the selling organisation. In order to get a feel for a ballpark figure, I asked the sales director what the initial order would be worth. 'Oh,' he said cheerfully, 'The first order will be about £280 million, but the total deal over three years will amount to the thick edge of £1 billion.' Truly this was big ticket selling, and I was in some awe of a team that would take on such a task. Remember, if they lost, they would get nothing and the company would almost certainly have to close the factories geared up to make the products.

On another occasion I sat in on a meeting where a salesman sold a manager a Web site and the expertise to set it up and keep the site up to date. At its lowest this was going to cost about £1500 and at most £3000. Yet the process the salesman had to use was the same as the process for the telecommunications team.

If, however, you look at how computer component salespeople work in the component distribution business, you will see that they sell on price and availability. After all, the actual products they are distributing are exactly the same as those of their competitors. So they work on developing sound and friendly relationships with their customers, but never try to think of something new they might do with the components they buy in. And yet, in terms of value, they can be taking very large orders indeed.

So, I conclude, big ticket selling is a misnomer. It is not just the value of the order that chooses the selling method, it is the need to discover what impact the product or service you are selling will have on the prospect, knowing that this will be different from every other customer you have sold to, and will also be different from the customer's original expectation. The salesperson or sales team is adding to the value of the products and services being offered in the course of the sales campaign.

So, it is big ticket, it is different from selling fruit off a market stall but mainly it is about selling not a product or a service, but selling a solution to a problem or selling the ability of the customer to exploit an opportunity. In the words of an IT director, 'Choose to sell for a company with whose objectives you can identify, put yourself into the moccasins of your customers, and try to understand their business better than they do.' And you don't have to charge the thick edge of a billion pounds.

Idea 49 – Sell high

The topic of level of contact is frequently discussed by selling teams. This is not surprising, as it is probably the most difficult thing to get right in solution selling. Imagine that you are selling a service that has a technical content, heating and ventilation say, as well as financial ramifications.

In this sort of buying decision there will be the people who are doing the technical evaluation work, and those who will agree that the evaluation should happen and decide the outcome.

While you are bound to spend a lot of time with the evaluators, it is vital to retain regular contact with the other group of decision makers. This can be a political minefield. Most people have been told at some time or other: 'If you go above my head and sell to my boss I will make sure that you play no more part in this evaluation.'

A variation on this is: 'There is no purpose in your meeting the senior people, they will merely rubber-stamp my recommendation.' In both of these cases someone, often the technical buyers, are acting as gatekeepers and preventing the selling team having access to decision makers.

Once again you have to plan how you are going to prove the added value of having this access. You will not always succeed, but you have to try. Why?

First, you need a statement from the top if you are going to understand the context of the proposed project. You need to hear the senior managers express what they regard as important in order to aim your proposal at the heart of their business. Second, you avoid the internal politics of the buying company, and third, you get some control of the whole buying cycle.

Here's a good, though unintentional, example of this. When I was a rookie salesperson, I attended a meeting that included the great Jules Thorn, the founder of Thorn EMI and currently its head. I thought no more of it until I visited the managing director of one of his subsidiaries. I mentioned that meeting and the effect was electric. The MD came forward in his seat, 'You've just met Jules Thorn,' he gasped, 'Did he mention my business?' I had inadvertently revolutionised my credibility and control with this customer.

So, 'screw your courage to the sticking place,' and go in high.

A relationship with a senior individual can in some cases be the lifeblood of a struggling new business. I know of one company with a leading-edge product who sold it into a major local authority. Through a combination of the technical difficulties of the product, a surge in deliveries to other companies and some pure bad luck, the implementation went very badly. Not only very badly but also very visibly. Like there were very long queues of angry ratepayers, they're also voters don't forget, outside the authority's housing offices.

This went on in all for some eighteen months. Just as the implementation was correcting itself the MD of the selling company heard distressing news right from the top. The director of finance was taking a particular interest in the problems and had asked for a copy of the contract to study. The MD, who had met and developed a relationship with the director of finance, picked up the phone and arranged to meet him. By asking some probing questions the seller discovered that the cause of the finance woman's discomfort was not so much the belated contribution of the equipment, but the fact that she had signed a contract that only guaranteed that the selling company would maintain the equipment for five years. She could foresee having to go to the elected members after three and a bit years to start the process of ordering replacement machines. And this would be before they had forgotten all about the implementation problems. The MD was able to extend the maintenance contract for another two years and by so doing satisfy the director of finance. Not only that but he did a good deal for his company by getting the extension contract paid for up-front, thus solving the customer satisfaction problem and a nasty cash situation in one shot. Now, if he had not had access to and a good relationship with the top person? It does not bear thinking about. Local authorities have lawyers – legions of them.

Idea 50 – Sell wide

Width of contact is also important. Classic solution selling means touching base with anyone who may at some point become involved in the decision-making process. Watch out for lawyers and finance people. They often appear towards the end of the buying cycle and stick a terms and conditions spanner in the works. Seek them out early and by so doing neutralise them or come to a swift conclusion that you cannot do business with them.

At the end of any business-to-business sales campaign some poor person in the buying company has to implement what was bought. These people, the users, bear the pain of the change that any new way of doing things causes, and are responsible for producing the benefits that the supplier's proposal offered. They are not necessarily the technical people, they are necessarily not the top people, but they are very important to the selling team as they have to agree that what is being proposed is achievable and that they will happily take on the implementation tasks. So court them widely in your target company.

Idea 51 – Sell the right benefits to the right person

Make sure the benefits of your solution are relevant to the person to whom you are proposing them. You will often see examples of irrelevant benefit selling particularly if the 'establishing need' part of the selling cycle has been poorly carried out.

A frequent investment that companies make is in improving their distribution systems. They buy automated warehouses, new fleets of vehicles or new computer systems but the aim in each case is the same – to physically possess their products for as short a time as possible. The measure of success of all of these improvements is the resulting change in stock turnover. This is a ratio of stock held to sales turnover. Some people quote it as the number of times stock is turned over in a year, others by the number of days stock is held either in vehicles or in a warehouse or factory. How do you sell this benefit?

When selling to the accountants the experienced salesperson will emphasise the reduction in the amount of stock held, since that is a relatively concrete outcome that the company can control.

The same argument expressed to sales directors will lead to despairing cries of, 'But we cannot give our customers what they want in the timescale they require it with the *current* levels of stock. Don't make it worse.' The benefit of improved stock control for sales directors comes from increased sales caused by the better availability of stock due to the new investment.

In actuality the benefits will be a mixture of the two, decreased stocks in some areas and more sales in others. Perhaps the mixture is the right way to sell to the managing director.

Don't forget that benefits have a personal edge. Selling a big productivity hike to the person in charge of the people who will be let go as the result of your project is probably not good tactics, unless you show that you and your company can bring real help to him or her as they face the redundant staff and their loss of empire.

Keep asking the 'so-what?' question:

- My solution has this feature. *So what?*
- You will be able to make do with one truck less. *So what?*
- Your people will get more job satisfaction if they do it this way. *So what?*

It is the answer to this question, in relation solely to the person you are talking to, that identifies the real benefit of your proposal.

Idea 52 – Qualification is a continuous process

There is a Chinese proverb that states, 'Before you decide where you want to go and how you are going to get there, make sure you know exactly where you are now.' In business-to-business selling you have to add, 'and make sure everyone involved agrees'. Your requirement is to produce a template of the feelings and situation of a customer who will buy from you. The process to do this is qualification. It is more complex than qualifying a consumer prospect, but it is as important to do it in team planning as it is to check that your prospect has a dog if you are selling pet insurance.

Some would regard this part of the planning process as the most important. The qualification process never stops. Professional account managers and sales people are constantly assessing the changing position in the campaign. They are listening for signs, sometimes obvious, sometimes subtle, which tell them how they stand against the competition.

What follows is the description of a checklist which probes into the areas where salespeople need to ask hard questions and acknowledge the answers, even those that say that all is not going well.

Let us assume you are selling a complex solution to a complex problem and that you have a team of technicians and business knowledge experts involved in the campaign. We will look at the process under the following headline questions:

- customer need;
- finance;
- key people;
- timescale;
- solution;
- basis of decision;
- implementation practicality; and
- competitive position.

Taking each of these one by one, we will look at the subsidiary questions in each heading and use examples from a number of situations.

There is a Chinese proverb that states, 'Before you decide where you want to go and how you are going to get there, make sure you know exactly where you are now.' In business-to-business selling you have to add, 'and make sure everyone involved agrees'.

Customer need

In this section the team examines what progress has been made on the completion of a business case for the customer on which he could make a decision to buy. The subsidiary questions are as follows:

Is it a real need?
The professional seller is well aware that all managers and technicians are interested in new things. The purchasing department of a large retailer will include people who are constantly monitoring the market and the suppliers to it for new products.

Computer and telecommunications people at all levels are notorious for looking into new technologies, studying them until they understand them and then dropping their interest as soon as something which is two keystrokes better comes along.

Selling teams are on their guard for timewasters, and this question is a good starting point for establishing whether or not the prospect is seriously going to contemplate what you are proposing.

The best test is: 'If you, the selling team, were running your customer's business, would you buy this product and go into this new environment?' If the answer to this is 'Yes' then you have the start of a qualified prospect. If the customer at high level also expresses a real need for the solution, you have the beginnings of a real runner.

A new technology is particularly difficult to get past this simple test. The fact is that if a company to date has found no need for a smart card which can also be used to dial telephone numbers, then you are going to have to persuade a lot of executives to take the initial risk.

Is the requirement strategic to the customer?
The work that the team has done in assessing the customer's business situation will tell it the strength of its situation in this regard. If the team can identify and sell the link between the project and the customer's strategy, the team will score well here.

Here is an example of a team swallowing the pill of a difficult qualifying decision.

An advertising agency put a lot of effort into a bid for the business of the Singapore subsidiary of a global pharmaceuticals and chemicals company.

The team members had failed to understand that pharmaceuticals were no longer a strategic business to the corporation. They could have known this, had they studied the published information or spoken to some senior managers at head office. What they could not know was that the corporation was actively seeking a buyer for the pharmaceutical subsidiary.

In any case this was a very difficult campaign to qualify, as the team would have had to understand the strategic aims of the account and then acted on it by dropping the campaign or slimming down their effort to a holding position. Probably under pressure from the Singapore company itself to make an offer, the decision to drop out of the sale becomes even harder.

They continued to put the effort in, took the client to meet satisfied customers, made a proposal and laid on a professional and expensive presentation.

The bombshell dropped with the announcement that the corporation was involved in friendly talks with a possible buyer and all activities except the day-to-day continuation of trading were halted.

Is the campaign worth the necessary effort from the selling company?
This is the crunch. From the team's understanding of the customer's position and attitude to going forward with the project, it has to make a go or no-go decision. Not only that, but it has to revisit that decision on a regular basis as the customer's stance develops and changes.

In summary, identifying a real need for the customer to act on strategically is the strongest basis for a sales campaign, and the absence of that is the weakest.

Finance

Is the money available in a budget?
Depending on the level of the customer you are dealing with, you need to find out

how budgets are set and whether some money is or could be allocated to the project you are selling.

Frequently, large companies have capital investment budgets separate from the day-to-day running budgets or revenue budgets. If it is possible, it is very desirable for the selling team to know how these budgets are set and to what level they are delegated.

The delegation issue is important. Some boards will delegate portions of the capital investment budget to the next level of management, but insist that each major item of expenditure returns to them with a report and a recommendation on which they will then make a decision.

Other boards will actually delegate the decision to the next level, or even lower. The trend as I write is towards more centralised control of capital expenditure budgets.

Having established where the budgets are, the selling team then has to answer the question: 'Has money been allocated to this project?' Or, failing that, 'Is there a reasonable chance that the money can be found?'

Be careful of a referral to another level. A salesperson was selling to the product development manager of a firm of stockbrokers. He carefully established that the manager concerned did have the authority to sign for a pilot scheme of £20,000. The budget was his and he had sufficient in his research and development fund to allocate the money to this project.

Unfortunately, he did not have the budget to fund the full project which, when the solution was rolled out to all customers, was going to cost some £100,000. His boss took the view that a decision on the pilot could only be taken if the people responsible for the larger amount were consulted and their agreement sought.

The result was much delay while the selling team demonstrated and sold the product to the sales and marketing department.

This was very difficult for the selling team to discover in the qualification process, but is a good example of how careful and wide you have to be in your questioning in this area.

Do all the people concerned have a rough cost expectation?
It is important to let everyone involved know what the cost of a project is likely to be. This sub question records whether or not the selling team has grasped the nettle or ducked the issue.

Once again level of contact plays its part. It is not enough to find one manager who sees no problem in the money being found. Many salespeople have been blind-sided by a senior manager stepping in at the last moment or at any time in the campaign with the dreaded question 'How much?' said in a tone of disbelief.

Has the necessary return on investment process been completed?
In the qualification process this question is a summary of the customer's attitude to return on investment. Unusually it is a yes or no answer.

A large company will almost certainly have a business process for examining return on investment. With or without the selling company's knowledge the buying company will put new projects through this process. The team needs to identify the key person on the buying side who is responsible for this and ask the direct question, 'Has the project been evaluated, and did it pass?'

In fact the seller may very well be able to add value to the evaluation process because of his or her knowledge of other companies who have gone down the same route. A professional sales person may be able to suggest costs that the buying team has not identified or, more importantly, assist the buying team to assess or quantify the benefits of the proposition.

Key people

We have already discussed the importance of level of contact, and this question in the qualification checklist records your progress in this area. You need to answer the following questions.

Do you know all the key people?

Even just making the initial list can be hazardous. In discussion with your main contact you should get fairly close to who is going to be involved. However, what you are looking for is who the decision maker will turn to for an authoritative opinion on some aspect of the project.

The more people involved, the harder the campaign. The higher the individuals in the organisation, the more difficult it will be to get regular contact with them.

The definition of this question is, 'Can we when we need it, get access to anyone involved from the customer's side in the process of evaluation?'

If the project is big enough or important enough to the buying company, this could be a lot of people. I was involved with a campaign where the selling team identified 50 people who would have some influence and involvement in the evaluation process.

Do we have as good access to the key people as your competitors do?

Here is another litmus test. In some cases you will not succeed in getting contact with all the people involved. This second test then becomes crucial. You are on a very uneven playing pitch if the competition is talking to people to whom you do not have access. If these people happen to be the most senior managers in the buying organisation this could be critical to your hopes of success. If you remember my golden rule of qualification – 'If a part of your campaign could be going wrong, it probably is' – you will pay enough attention to competitive level of contact to ensure that you are not fighting the bidding battle with a considerable handicap.

Timescale

If the key-people question is one of the most important, then the timescale question is one of the most difficult to answer authoritatively. The human condition leads, in the main, to avoiding change and postponing decisions. A professional solution-seller is almost all the time proposing significant change and suggesting that a decision is made soon and urgently.

Have the key people agreed a decision date?
People are frequently reluctant to make a firm date on which they will make a buying decision. There is no magic answer. If in the end a customer decides to postpone a decision or a project, that is his prerogative. All the salesperson can do is persistently probe for the feasibility of a decision date.

In pursuing the timescale question, salespeople are also checking that the customer is actually in a position to buy. The credibility of a sales forecast depends on the degree to which the salesperson can convince his or her manager that the customer is realistically in a position to go ahead.

Ask the question early in the campaign, for example at the first meeting. People are happier to take a commitment when the date of delivering that commitment is a long way off. It is easier to get an agreed date in three months time, than to try and tie someone down to making a decision next week.

Is there an agreed implementation timescale?
However clever a product is and however much a customer needs it, the solution suggested by the product must be buyable and implementable.

There is a great opportunity to get the competitive edge of being the first salesperson to work with the customer to produce the outline of an implementation plan, sometimes described as 'timetable' selling. During the opening call with a prospect or customer on a particular campaign, a professional seller will try to get them to assist with the creation of a bar chart identifying all the major milestones in the implementation of the proposed project.

The modification of this forms part of all subsequent calls and, of course, the requirement for a decision date to be part of the implementation plan is clear.

Solution

So far the emphasis in the qualification process has been on buyability. We need now to turn to the sellability side. The business of your dreams is concerned with the long-term relationship with a customer, which in turn is concerned with delivering customer satisfaction time after time after time.

The proposed solution should have a number of attributes. First and foremost it must solve the problem or assist the customer to exploit the opportunity. Next it must represent good business for the selling company. The main measures for this are profitability and risk.

The three subsidiary questions are:

Is your solution valid?
It is unlikely in a complex project that any solution offered will meet every single detail of the customer's specification. Most decisions of this nature have some compromise built in. The key for the selling team is to ensure the validity of its offering and agree this with the customer.

Is the risk of your being able to deliver your promises acceptable?
Insist that the people in your team who are responsible think through the implementation carefully. After all, we don't want to bet the firm.

Is the project profitable now or through future sales?
In complex selling you must make an estimated profit and loss account for each individual project. You will have to, of course, if your sales people are motivated by selling gross margin. The level of profit required will obviously vary project by project. At the most profitable end will be repeats of previous sales of high-value products; while at the low end will be loss leaders where the whole reason for the sale is that other orders will flow from this one.

Basis of decision

Establishing the basis of decision is said by many to be the key technique separating the solution seller from the product salesperson or box shifter. It involves understanding from the customer's point of view all the issues surrounding the sale.

Have you agreed with the key people their criteria for deciding to go ahead?
Ask and keep asking, so that by the time it comes to making your proposal you can put it in their terms, not only from the business case point of view, but also for all the key issues that surround the buying decision and the implementation.

Have you influenced this?
Try to get the customer to agree from his point of view the reasons why he will buy. This is much more powerful selling than just hitting them with features and benefits.
    The difference is between the following two statements:

• *Aren't the people in the warehouse going to prefer to keep the same shelf layout even when the new system comes along?* and
• *If you buy the system I am selling you will not have to change the shelf layout.*

The first is seeking to agree a criterion for decision making. The second is simply a statement of a feature.
    In the end, of course, the basis of decision that includes a feature or issue that is unique to one of the selling companies tilts the balance firmly in their favour.

Implementation practicality

Assess how well you are organised to ensure an efficient implementation. Examine the resource requirement that will result in a successful project from both sides' point of view.

There are three sub-questions.

Are the customer's implementation resources available and allocated to this project?
Once again the professional solution seller is being upfront with what the customer is going to have to do. A resource deficiency or skill absence should offer to the seller an opportunity rather than a threat.

Are you prepared to put in the resources required to carry out the campaign plan?
To begin with, the answer to this will be 'No'. It is not until you have worked out the plan and its resource implications that the answer to this question can become positive.

Are the implementation support resources from your side identified and allocated?
If you are to be convincing in your presentation of how the project will succeed if the buyer says 'Yes', you need to know that your support will be available at the time it will be needed.

Competitive position

All the qualification work which has gone before should allow the team to answer the crucial question of whether or not they are likely to win this business against the competition.

The biggest waste of any salesperson's time is the time spent on bids and tenders that are then lost. At the end this is what qualification is about: 'Am I spending my own and my team's time wisely? Is there anywhere else that this time could be more profitably used?'

Can you identify one or more areas where you have competitive advantage?
Without this, the team is selling on price. That is, if all other things are equal, the

buying team will choose the cheapest bid. This is an unacceptable situation and the selling team must try to establish some feature of its offering which distinguishes it from the competition.

Whatever the area, find your competitive edge, so that in the action plan part of the campaign-planning process, you can work out how to exploit that edge.

So that's it, the qualification process in a nutshell. You and your team will already be doing much of it as a matter of normal business. The great idea is to formalise it and make your own tailored process from the general template described above.

Idea 53 – Use radar to plot your position

It is very useful to present the qualification checklist as a radar diagram which, because of its appearance, I call the *spider's web*.

Here is an example:

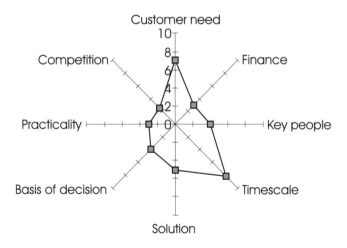

The rationale could look like this:

- *Customer need (score 7)*
  There is a good *prima facie* requirement that is agreed by the decision maker to be strategically desirable. It will be well worth our effort. The only problem here is that we do not understand the process for deciding on return on investment.
- *Finance (score 3)*
  The decision maker has said that he will make the money available, if his people come to him with a business case. It is not in a budget yet.
- *Key people (score 4)*
  We know who the key people are, but have no further access to the decision maker until the time of proposal. The technical recommender, who is taking the lead, is trying to block us from the user recommenders.
- *Timescale (score 8)*
  Good news here as the timescale is driven by a product launch which the customer is planning as a key date. The pressure on the launch date comes from legislation, so it is highly unlikely to be postponed.
- *Solution (score 5)*
  We have done this sort of thing many times before, but we are going to have to work with a third party with whom we have had no dealings. Once we agree the way ahead with the third party, the situation should improve.
- *Basis of decision (score 4)*
  We do not know the financial basis of decision. The technical basis is clear but contains no unique reason why they should buy from us. Our lack of contact with the user recommenders means that we do not understand the practical issues to be covered.
- *Implementation practicality (score 3)*
  It is a bit early in the campaign to be able to allocate resources. On the face of it does not look too difficult.

- *Competitive position (score 2.5)*
  There are four competitors bidding and we have no reason to think that we are better or worse placed than any other.

In time, planning teams will start to see patterns in their spider's webs that they can recognise. You can also use the spider's web as a presentation aid when describing the state of a sales campaign to a manager or other interested party.

Some companies have put the spider's web into their culture. They have familiarised everyone with the concept so that there is a completely consistent approach to qualification and briefings.

Five Greatest Ideas for Managing Your Bank

Introduction

I was heavily involved with bank managers back in the eighties when a business school hired me to run some marketing (i.e. selling) courses. In the end we agreed that if I had succeeded in persuading most of them to smile at the customers rather than spit at them I had done a reasonable job. Now I know things have changed and banks are probably more customer-friendly now, but I guess my prejudice is well set. In fact one of my current small-business customers finds their local bank manger very useful, supportive and interested in their business and their success. Other people I know are not so lucky. In case he is reading this, can I just say that our bank manager at the moment is first rate?

Anyway, your relationship with your banker is important, so lets look at some great ideas for building the lender of your dreams.

Idea 54 – Get the basics right

One of the contributors to this book went into a conversation with two business people who were masters of their trade, but whose business sense made the visitor reel. The situation was that they owed some £750,000 in an overdraft whose actual limit was £700,000. They had their houses at risk as guarantees against the bank lending, and they were, to say the least, worried.

Looking around at the end of February the entrepreneur discovered that no one had sent out January's invoices. Not only that but there were amounts in debtors well overdue. The explanation was that they were too busy trying to deliver service to a big customer in a contract that was worth a lot of money, and eventually cash. But that cannot be right. Make sure that invoices happen as soon as possible, that your collection terms are known by and agreed by your clients and put someone in charge of keeping the system up to date and chasing debt. Lots of companies simply do not pay their bills until someone chases for payment. Get payment up front whenever you can.

Idea 55 – KISS and TICK

You will have heard the expression KISS – '*keep it simple, stupid*' – and it is without doubt good advice. In the end, trading is about two people representing two organisations offering a deal – 'If you do this, I will do that.' Try to keep your business focused on that simple concept.

TICK is the other key acronym for the person with his or her own business. It stands for '*think in cash, knucklehead*'. Remember the mantra, 'Profit is opinion, cash is reality' and make sure that you have a firm grip on that reality. Companies do not actually go out of business because they run out of profits; Eurotunnel and many high-technology businesses have not made a profit yet, but are still very much in business. No, companies go out of business because they run out of cash. So when you are starting, keep your projected cashflow up to date on at least a weekly basis.

What you are trying very hard to avoid with your bank manager is giving him or her a surprise of any sort. There are two reasons for this. Firstly if you suddenly pitch up for the third time in a year needing more borrowings immediately because you will run out of cash when you pay this week's wages bill, the bank may very well call it a day. Their grounds for calling in the loans at that point could be that they simply do not believe that you have what it takes to control a business, and they want out while the assets can still be sold or your house still covers the outstanding borrowings.

The other reason for never giving them a surprise is that they are basically free at that point to charge you whatever they like. Think of them this way. If someone offered to lend you £10 for a week, but asked you to agree to pay back twice that amount at the time of repayment, you would not need to have read this book to realise that that is a bad deal. Suppose, however, that you are completely broke and know that you will have £71 in cash by the day at which you have to make the capital and 100% interest repayment – still not interested? Ah, I forget to mention that your two children have not eaten for 36 hours and that they are wailing for food. In such circumstances the loan sharks of the inner-city sink estates make such loans and prosper. This is a suitable and accurate starting point for thinking about the purveyors of loan capital.

Their view is that they tailor their interest charges to protect themselves against the risk of default. The more difficult the situation the borrower is in, the higher the risk and therefore the higher the price of help.

If you are running a huge conglomerate and wish to borrow $250 million to buy up a subsidiary in another country, you will be wined and dined by various money-lenders eager to get your business at less than 1% above the rate at which the banks themselves borrow money. If you need £20,000 to tide your corner shop over a refurbishment, you will probably have to trawl the High Street to find a lender willing to lend you the money at 5 or 6% above bank rate. And they will probably want you to back the security of the loan by re-mortgaging your house. Banks are indeed the people who lend umbrellas to small businesses only when it is not raining.

So don't give them any surprises by the consistent use of KISS and TICK.

Idea 56 – Keep your cashflow document up to date

Producing a good cashflow statement depends on four things, one of which should be easy, the second gets easier with time, the third takes up much more time than you could possibly imagine and the fourth is a bastard. They are:

1. An accurate estimate of your fixed costs: when you did your documentation for the bank, you will have filled out the expenses and wages sheet that identifies your fixed costs. As you add to them, keep this number up to date. Remember

this is a cashflow so you do not include any depreciation that comes off your monthly profit and loss account. If you are depreciating fixed assets such as computer equipment, for example, the cash implication will be under capital expenditure on the week that you buy the equipment or in fixed costs as loan repayments if that is how you financed it. Its value, remember, is an opinion, we are only interested in the reality.

2. Variable costs: costs that only occur when you make products or deliver services. The cashflow will include the details of the money spent on production as it occurs. If you sell the services of consultants but they are on your books, then you should include them in fixed costs – you have to pay for them whether they are working or not. If you employ casual labour depending on having work for them, then you will have to become good at estimating your profit margin as you sell them on. So a building contractor will take a view on the percentage of sales that comes through as variable costs. It will not be very accurate but there will be sufficient compensating errors if you work on the conservative side to ensure a reasonably true picture. Think hard about your variable costs and improve your ability to estimate them and understand the timing of payments.

3. Your skills in getting your bills paid: don't underestimate how much time needs to be spent on it, and spend money on a resource to do it for you if it is taking up too much of your time.

4. And finally the bastard: the top line of a cashflow is the sales forecast, the most difficult estimate of them all. Not only do you have to guess how many units you will sell, you also have to estimate when the orders and deliveries will happen. Add to this the problem that you might not get all the orders you bid for because you will lose some to the competition. You know you will lose some, but which ones?

Here is an example of a fairly rough and ready cashflow for a contractor with various levels of gross margin. It was prepared by an expert contractor rather than an accountant who might find it a bit inelegant; but it does the job. Management can see what needs to be done to ensure a satisfactory cash position.

Income from current debtors @ 6 Dec	Total	Dec	Jan	Feb	Mar	April	May	June	July	Notes
										1
Customer 1	30000	30000								
Customer 2	3300	3300								
Customer 3	11500	6000	5500							2
Customer 4	14000	7000	7000							
Customer 5	5500	1500	4000							
Insurance claim	3000			3000						
Others	2000	1000	1000							
Debtor income	**69300**	**48800**	**17500**	**3000**						3

Expected sales	Value	Dec	Jan	Feb	Mar	April	May	June	July
Customer 6	132000		13000	44000	30000	45000			
Others	31000	31000	0	0	0	0	0		
Total sales	**163000**	**31000**	**13000**	**44000**	**30000**	**45000**	**0**		

Sales receipts		Dec	Jan	Feb	Mar	April	May	June	July	Notes
	Debtors	48800	17500	3000						
From sales	30 days		15500	6500	22000	15000	22500	0		4
From sales	60 days			15500	6500	22000	15000	22500	0	
Total receipts	**232300**	**48800**	**33000**	**25000**	**28500**	**37000**	**37500**	**22500**	**0**	

		Dec	Jan	Feb	Mar	April	May	June	July	Notes
Fixed costs		11000	11000	11000	11000	11000	11000	11000	11000	5
Cost of sales										
Customer 6 @ 20% mark-up					10833	36667	25000	37500		
						0	0	0	0	
Other @ 20% mark-up			20000	25833	0	0	0	0	0	
Total outgoing		**11000**	**31000**	**36833**	**21833**	**47667**	**36000**	**48500**	**11000**	6

Cashflow balance	Dec	Jan	Feb	Mar	April	May	June	July
Bank	0							
Add sales receipts	48800	33000	25000	28500	37000	37500	22500	0
Reduce by outgoing costs	11000	31000	36833	21833	47667	36000	48500	11000
Cash position	**37800**	**2000**	**-11833**	**6666.7**	**-10667**	**1500**	**-26000**	**-11000**
Cumulative	37800	39800	27967	34633	23967	25467	-533.3	-11533

Balance @ end of July -11533

Notes

1 The doubtful payer is not shown.
2 Uninvoiced retentions of £25K not shown, part of which will be incoming over the period shown.
3 Receipts from current debtors are agreed payment dates.
4 Sales receipts assumed to take: 50% 60 days; 50% 30 days.
5 Staff numbers assumed to remain the same.
6 Creditors are assumed to be stretched up to 60 days.

Review this on at least a monthly basis. Do it weekly if you are managing a difficult situation. The trick is to generate one that reflects your business very well, and needs little work to update it. Doing it without a spreadsheet on a computer is truly doing it the hard way.

Idea 57 – Smile until your face aches

Your relationship with your banker is at least as crucial as your relationship with your biggest customer. The aiming point can be described as follows: When you make a mistake (inevitable) or when one of your payers lets you down either by delaying a payment or going bust (very likely), you need to be able to turn to your bank manager, tell him or her a version of what has happened and have them step in with the necessary short-term or long-term cash to solve the problem at a more reasonable price than if he or she did not like or trust you.

Your relation-ship with your banker is at least as crucial as your rela-tionship with your biggest customer.

How do you do it? Keep them in the picture. Make presentations to them with properly prepared visual aids with their names on them, to show that you have taken effort to present your affairs as accurately as possible. Demonstrate that your finger is firmly on the cash button. Smile a lot and show confidence that the thing will come through in the end, even if you have not slept much for a while. Take them out to lunch to 'thank them' when something you were forecasting actually comes through. Don't take them to an expensive customer hospitality event just after you lose a big order, and so on. You plan the relationship with your biggest customer don't you? So do it with your banker too.

Idea 58 – Go for as much as you can get

Having a big borrowing facility is very useful, so go for as much of a facility as you can get that will cover your requirements much more than adequately. It has only one down side, and that is that you have to pay a percentage of the full facility each year for the privilege whether you take the money up or not. It has several up sides:

- If something goes wrong, it means that you can borrow your way out of the problem without having to explain everything to the bank manager at the same time.
- Your bank manger will see your prudence in having a buffer matched by your efficiency in never having to use it.
- If an opportunity arises where you need to move quickly, for example taking over another business, the bank would otherwise be another professional you have to brief on what you are doing. If their role is not changed in the new circumstances you have saved time and hassle.
- If you have a facility to borrow but are not using it, it might just make you think about other things that you could do. But if the only thing you can think of is to buy better cars for the directors, then you may just discover another downside of borrowing more than you need.

Five Greatest Ideas for Running the Board Effectively

Introduction

The role of a director at the top, or holding-company level is different from that of a manager. You have to have the confidence to go into this new role knowing that you have much to learn. But you have your reputation as a manager behind you, so all you have to do is learn the new roles, *Idea 63*, and think about all the people involved with the board. But let us start with a valuable lesson derived from a person who started on a board that was not true to themselves and discovered the importance of *Idea 59*.

Idea 59 – Keep an honest boardroom

There is absolutely no place in the boardroom for dishonesty, particularly of the sort that pretends there is no problem where there actually is. Suppose you are planning a new initiative. You have researched the product market, decided on your competitive strategy and the only thing left to do is make it happen. Now ask yourselves 'Do we have the knowledge and experience in this room to manage this project?'

If it involves, for example, the entrepreneur on the board managing a new group of staff who do a repetitive job and suffer from low morale, you may want to think again. Try not to put anyone, including yourself, into the position of doing something they are not good at. This requires the honesty of everyone to admit or volunteer gaps in their skills or knowledge.

Look at it this way. When you had appraisals in big companies they will have confirmed your brilliance in some areas and 'need for development' in others. You probably tried to eliminate these weaknesses, and indeed probably convinced your boss that you had. But they remain your weaker areas. Everyone has varying degrees of skill and competence in certain aspects of their business and indeed personal lives and what you are good and bad at is blatantly obvious to your colleagues.

So, don't cover it up. Surround yourself with people with complementary skill sets and encourage them to be as honest as you and to be confident in the things they do well.

Idea 60 – Give your non-executive directors huge credence

You will choose your non-executive directors for something that they bring to the party. It may be contacts, market knowledge, industry experience or whatever; but it is new to this boardroom. Now get it clear 'What does the board need?' and make sure that the non-exec is clear about their contribution. Then listen to them.

If they are experienced directors amongst less experienced colleagues, then do not just listen to what they say about the particular area you brought them in for, but listen to them as well on anything to do with the responsibilities and roles of the board. You are learning these and making them up as you go along. They actually know what works.

I once had a great row with a non-executive director who was immensely experienced at board level having worked with a venture capital firm as a non-exec for several of their investments. The problem was 'cost of sales' in a consultancy-oriented company. He wanted monthly information on cost of sales. That is, he wanted to know what the consultants and materials we had supplied that month had actually cost. I insisted that the consultants were in any case part of the fixed costs, and that it was therefore a waste of time to keep that cost of sales information. It's embarrassing to write it down now, it being so obvious that he was right, but I did sort of have a point. In the end we listened to him, or rather I was forced by the chief executive to listen to him, changed the data recording system so that it gave us that information and gained a number of excellent insights into the business as a result.

Unfortunately in this company when it came to a disagreement between the chief executive and the non-exec it was not possible to get the chief executive, a man from the North whose management style was akin to that of a nineteenth-century mill owner, to change his mind, and the company lost the non-exec. The issue was the number of times the board should meet, with the chief executive, who was plainly starting to find the meetings a hindrance to his getting his own way, trying to cut the number down. In the end the company did not meet anyone's dreams, although it gave us all a good living for a while, and became more or less a sole proprietorship partly because of this failure to listen to the voice of experience and knowledge.

If your people are indeed the greatest asset that you have then treat them right, since logically they are a huge source of competitive edge – they are unique.

Idea 61 – Do regular stakeholder analysis

Most companies have four stakeholders: customers, suppliers, shareholders and staff. (Bankers would probably want to add lenders who are not shareholders, but bankers are tedious and common so they can shut up.) You should regularly review how your business is treating each of these. Ask yourself what would these people say about your company.

There is much in this book about the customer issues; so suffice it to say that company-wide review of the treatment of your customers is vital.

Suppliers will give better service to customers with whom it is easy to do business. Look for ways that you can help them with their problems and keep your relationship and transactions with them as simple as possible. You never know when they might come up with the killer idea that makes you, as well as them, rich.

If your people are indeed the greatest asset that you have then treat them right, since logically they are a huge source of competitive edge – they are unique. Don't fudge soft issues such as job satisfaction and development and training. Put hard measures in place to make sure that you are taking these as seriously in actions as you are in words. It is unlikely that a human resources department will be cost-effective until you are a fair size. In any case your managers should carry out most of what the HR department would do, and for the technical issues, tax and cars and so on, use your accountant until he or she is stretched to carry out the role. At that point you may consider outsourcing the specialist bits, or, if you are growing rapidly get a headhunter to join the board as a non-exec.

Idea 62 – Choose the right accountants

Almost everyone I spoke to mentioned this. To be honest many of them had learnt by taking on the wrong one to begin with. The right accountant is a terrific asset, while the wrong one is potentially a huge liability. This gives us some clues to the best advice:

- Look for an accountant who is appropriate for your size of business. They are unlikely to be able to add industry knowledge because they have clients in your area of operation, but they can give you good advice based on experience of companies going through the same type of growing pains as you.
- From this we can gather that you must not be afraid to change your account-ant when he or she has become less appropriate. If you have grown to twenty or thirty people the accountant who is brilliant with start-up companies may no longer be right for you.
- As you change your geography too you may have to change to an accountant who is able to support your premises all in different locations.
- The time may come when you need the 'branding' of one of the big boys to assist you in raising finance or buying businesses. One person gave this advice. If you are going to an outfit like KPMG, choose an office that is local to you but not in one of the big business metropolises. Once again this is because the

local office away from the main trading centres will have more experience of smaller, growing businesses and also have more time for you. His example was to choose Liverpool rather than Manchester.

- Accountants basically charge time and materials for as much of their work as you will let them get away with. When you pick up the phone on them they are like your telephone company and charge by the minute. Negotiate a fixed cost for as much of the list of items they are going to perform as possible. Keep reminding them to tell you when you are asking them to do something that is not on the list but will cost extra.

- The fees for doing the due diligence part of an acquisition or merger is a difficult area. Fundamentally you do not have time to negotiate with them and they will charge you royally for their advice. You may very well have them working at nights and at weekends and they will charge accordingly. The only good news is that this money does not come out of the profits of the business when you have bought it, but comes off the goodwill at the time of acquisition.

Idea 63 – Understand your roles and responsibilities

There is a lot of legislation covering the roles and responsibilities of directors of both private and public limited companies. Make sure you have a passing knowledge of these. If one of your companies does fail and someone, anyone, has been involved in wrongdoing, you can have a blot on your escutcheon for a long time, and a reputation that never goes away. Pay attention to this at all times. Read the board minutes with a legal eagle eye, and you should not go wrong.

Ten Greatest Ideas for Building the Retail Business of Your Dreams

Introduction

One of the interesting things that happens when you become a freelance or set up your own business is that other people frequently confide in you their version of the business of their dreams. Often they are doing just that – dreaming, and have no intention of attempting to make it come true. (Indeed some people dream and are on the brink of taking the plunge for so long that one comes to the conclusion that they are super-glued to the diving board.)

Sometimes their dream, if they were to implement it, would in fact be a nightmare. (I mean, have you ever really thought through what it would be like to run a pub in the country? It would be like opening up your living room to the same people every night whether you like them or not. And there are no police and no brewery overlord to enforce the licensing laws, so these people will stay until they want to go. Oh, and your hours are nine in the morning until, say, midnight, and that's on a good day.)

Nonetheless, there are good opportunities for turning a hobby into a business. In this section we are going to take as an example the business that most dreamers think about – retailing or consulting about things that excite them. So, if you want to open your art gallery or antiques shop; or if your bent is towards designing and installing kitchens or gardens here are a few great ideas supplied by people who have done it and achieved a lifestyle that suited them with an income sufficient to support it and more than a glimmer of hope that it might, with the Chancellor's blessing, turn into a retirement pension vehicle as well.

Idea 64 – Get your attitude right

Face it, if you are going to open your art gallery in Bond Street, you will need a lot of capital and an encyclopaedic knowledge of the international art market. Even then, your lack of experience in the retail business will almost certainly be your, very expensive, downfall. We are not talking mega-corporations here, rather starting off with one shop in a less than centrally located area of town or village. Most dreamers have to make it happen with very little capital. And that seems to be the first clue; this is a long-term plan and a long-term commitment. Think ten years to the end of the project, and a first business plan of, say, three years. If your actions are dictated by short-term considerations you may get over the teething problems quite well, but struggle with the follow up. It is much better to know the next step in advance and concentrate on that.

If you use high-pressure selling technique, you will at best sell one thing to each person who comes into the shop. But they will not come back.

Some people say that knowing the exit strategy after the ten-year plan is important, others that such a plan will become clearer as time passes.

The only thing unanimously called a mistake in this regard was to have huge riches as the end game. The rewards may be huge, there is always a chance, but your first objective is to earn enough for the lifestyle you dream of.

Then ask yourself, 'Do I passionately want to do it?' The attribute that ties together all the successful people doing this is that there are strong positive reasons for turning their passion into a business as well as the negative reasons concerned with getting out of the rat race. You are going to have to sell things, it's not like working in a chemist shop; it's about getting to know your customers and helping them to buy. If you use high-pressure selling technique, you will at best sell one thing to each person who comes into the shop. But they will not come back. So the thing that sells for you is your knowledge and, dare I say it, love for the product. They buy because they trust you when you say, 'This is good, and has a good provenance.' That is how you will build up the essential customer relationships that provide repeat purchases, if you are in retail, or references to other customers if you are on the consultancy side.

Now, I said that running a country pub is more like a nightmare than a dream, but don't underestimate the time commitment to any retail business. You never know when this month's big customer will come through the door, so it has to be open when people expect it to be open and some other times as well. This means that you almost certainly need a partner. A partner with a similar passion is ideal, as is the family business. You also have to face the fact that taking holidays will always be difficult and in the early years impossible. Even after some time it will still be difficult to get away for more than a week. You will just never find someone to take over with the same background knowledge and commitment as you. After all, that is what you are selling.

Idea 65 – Exploit people already in the know

Right, you have jumped in or are about to jump in, so your learning curve needs to be very steep. You are going to eat drink and sleep your chosen subject all day every day. You read, you browse the Internet and you learn. It needs to be a fairly narrow field, since you want to be an expert as quickly as you can. A man who set up a gallery to sell prints flirted with sculpture since it was an associated art, but stopped when he realised that his learning time was being spread too thin. You will by definition already be knowledgeable when you start, but look for people who can give you shortcuts in making further progress. Lean particularly on anyone who is going to be a supplier to you and pick their brains. They know the business inside out and are somewhat motivated to help you since they want you for a customer. Exploit any other contacts as well; this is no time to be a shrinking violet. Wander into similar shops in other areas and talk to the owner. If they do not see you as direct competition they will almost certainly be pleased to help. After all, you would in their place. Oh, and read the trade press avidly.

Quite quickly you will be hardly aware of how much you really do know, which is why you will, at first, be surprised when you find that the person who looks after the shop for one day while you go to a wedding has done so much damage in such a short time.

I know one person who took his skills from his previous working life to an antique stall in Petticoat Lane. He had previously been in the money markets connecting buyers to sellers and depending for his profit on the margin between the two prices. Everyone knew when he started that he knew very little about antiques and we wondered how he would survive. The answer was his ability, learnt in the money markets, to remember exactly what he had paid for every individual item on a crowded stall, none of which had a price tag on it. This made him a lethal negotiator since he always looked very casual and never consulted documents or books. In the end he became an expert in a narrow field, took on a partner and managed a number of shops.

Idea 66 – Get the timing right

You know the water is warm, you are braced for the dive, so what are you waiting for?

There is a fundamental rule in business that risk and reward go hand in hand – the higher the risk the higher will be the reward however that is measured. This makes selecting the right time to go for your dream a two-edged sword. Suppose you have a £200,000 mortgage on your property, two children at school and another on the way and ends are only just meeting on a salary of £55,000 a year; at that time the risk of your dream making an unwelcome but enforced change to your standard of living is probably too high. But remember those people with super-glue on their feet and don't wait too long. I mean, seriously, if you have enough money from your early retirement package to live comfortably without working at all, are you really going to want to get up six days a week to run a village post office?

The timing is a matter of capital and resources. It is a question of weighing up your obligations to your dependants, saving enough capital to put some money in as shareholders' funds and going for it as soon as common sense tells you these things are in balance.

A lot of people succeeded in getting going by having one partner leaving work and starting the dream, while the other continued earning in their current job, worked for the dream during their time off and did not draw any money out of the new business.

Finally in terms of timing, think about the premises you will need. Any business is a mixture of creating a good strategy and business plan, operating efficiently and seizing opportunities. The right premises will tend to belong to the third of these. You will have an accurate idea of what you are looking for and in what area it could be, but it could take some time to find the ideal place. When it does appear it is a strange irony that the shop or the workshop, the millstone round your neck, could very well be the clincher for when to plunge in.

Idea 67 – To buy or not to buy

Do you buy premises or rent them? This is a difficult one since it brings another potential source of profit to the business – if you buy you may make a profit when you sell the premises. On the other hand if you are selling the business as a going concern it may make little difference to the value of the business whether the shop is purchased or rented.

Probably the best way of making the decision is as a straightforward financial test. Assume for the moment that all other things are equal; you will sell the same amount of goods from the shop however you occupy it – owner or tenant. Now make a five-year cashflow of the outgoings involved for each method. Get the insurance side right and the rates and other expenses. Now discount the cashflow for time, and arrive at the net present value of the two methods and decide on the better of the two. If you do not know how to do this, get your accountant to show you and don't leave his or her office until you can do it – it is the only sensible way to measure any form of return on investment and an absolutely essential skill for a builder of a dream business.

Idea 68 – Fix your costs and know your costs

The next golden rule after understanding discounted cashflows is to have the tightest possible grip on your fixed costs. Try to take any variances or guesswork out of this. Some people, for example, believe that it is worth paying a little more to have a fixed rate of interest if they are borrowing money. The benefit that makes it worthwhile is the complete removal of uncertainty. Interests rates may go mad, but your loan will be exactly the same for the period of the loan, and therefore the period of the plan.

When you know your fixed costs per month, or even per week to begin with, you are in control of your business. You know exactly what the customers need to pay for you to make a living. Your living expenses, if you have to draw them, are part of the fixed costs. If for the first six months you are going to live on your savings, it makes a more impressive spreadsheet for the bank manager to look as if you put six month's worth of drawings in as capital, knowing that you will take it out as salary over the period.

Idea 69 – Treat your customers as what they are – your purpose in life

'Everybody lives by selling something' is a quotation, not from a red-clawed industrialist, but from the author and poet Robert Louis Stevenson. Only your customers will enable you to fulfil your dreams. In the early stages you will have to spend a high proportion of your available cash on marketing. The guy who runs the art gallery told me 'Spend ten per cent of each year's revenues on marketing, at least to begin with.'

Your stationery and your logo are important. Spend time and, if necessary, money on them. Your business name should have the echo of a branding or a positioning. It should suggest almost that new customers have heard of you before. This is not 'passing off', which is illegal, but making sure that the associations that people have with the name are positive and relevant.

You are always looking for repeat business and references to new prospects. If you can sell your product off the Internet, do it. This means that customers, who were in your locale once, can buy from you from wherever in the world they find themselves. Advertise in places where potential customers might come from. Remember, people with an interest in your speciality will travel to meet with and deal with someone who knows what they are talking about. So don't limit your advertising to your local paper. If your real pleasure comes from the buying of the products, don't let that diminish the amount of time you spend on promoting the business and finding new customers.

Once you have found them, keep a detailed record of who they are and what their interests are as well as what they bought. You will be surprised how quickly you build a database of information that makes your next mailshot extremely well focused – 'One of those tiny Georgian teapots has come into my possession, shall I keep it for the next time you drop in?' This database is a major asset of the business, and if you are eventually going to sell the business as a going concern it will be a huge contributor to the value of the goodwill you have built up.

Talking about goodwill, it is hard to win but terribly easy to throw away. A good reputation pays huge dividends in terms of repeat business and new customers attracted by word of mouth. Set your quality sights very high. If a customer has a problem with a product, or even if they just don't like it, take it back or fix the problem, literally without question. Try, obviously, to get them to take something in exchange, but if they insist just give them their money back. It is quality and service you are selling, not the product itself. Use the best materials for display and packaging and make the place look welcoming. Your customers are used to being treated as people in a line, or as targets for smooth salespeople; shopping with you should be a different sort of experience. The opposite of pressure and intimidation is to leave them alone unless they ask for help and to go away when you have answered their question and they look as though they are going to move on to another product or even another shop. Remember, you are in this for the long haul; they will probably come back if they felt no pressure. Oh, and leave the door open whenever the weather allows it. This avoids any feeling of being trapped.

The shop will obviously change slowly as you sell items and bring in new stock, but a consensus of opinion says that you should make a point of changing the place dramatically from time to time. One person who sells rare books told me that it was his practice to start a collection of new offerings but keep them in a bottom drawer until he had a good display. This meant that he was possibly not selling the books as soon as he could, but it also meant that he could send out a mailshot inviting customers to come in and see the new display when the time came. He did this when the shop was otherwise closed, gave them a glass of wine and frequently did well.

One other person who sells a small number of quite highly priced goods made sure that on the counter there were a number of attractive but inexpensive related items, in this case postcards of well known paintings. This meant that everyone could buy something and was also a useful source of petty cash.

Idea 70 – Count your customers

Every sale you make, every business card you receive should be part of your customer database. Build it from the start and you will quite quickly and for ever have the most precious marketing tool of the lot – people who have an interest in your products, and know you or your business.

The owner of the art shop explained it like this.

'We started by collecting the Christmas card lists from all our friends on the basis that like attracts like. We added relevant people from my past business life, my wife's life as a teacher and entered all of these, about 550 records, into the Microsoft Word database. This is not ideal but what do you want – it's free if you have Word? This we called our prospect file. We then opened a visitor's book in the shop itself and encouraged people to sign it or throw their business card into a large, and quite attractive, glass jar. This added to the prospects file.

'As we sold things and got customers, we entered the details of the sale into an Excel spreadsheet that we call our customer file. Once again not brilliant software, but it seems fit for purpose and we will not change until we discover a major deficiency in it. We want to have the customers identified so that we can invite them to previews or for a glass of wine if we have something interesting to show them. It is also useful to be able to scan the file and see who is buying what.

'We have stopped trying to guess exactly who will become customers because we still get so many surprises. All that means is that you must never throw any name away. Currently we have 1000 people on our prospect file and 500 customers. Combined with a good web page to which we can refer them from time to time, these give us a lot of our sales.'

Idea 71 – Diversify carefully

Once you have your premises, it is tempting to put them to greater use than just your original idea. There will, in fact, be no shortage of people offering to let you sell their wares through your shop for a percentage. Make sure that the wooden replicas hand-turned at a local crafts factory do not include a Trojan horse. We have covered one reason for looking at diversification with a sceptical eye – you really ought to learn as much about the new products as the old. After all, that is what you sell. There are other reasons:

- You must consider the use of the shelf space. Would it not make more sense to increase the stock of your main line of business? Granted that costs money, and they will let you display their toys for free, but that is what you are in business to do, buy more stock or stock of higher value. Besides, whatever the deal with your new supplier is bound to cost money in some way, and they will want their cash immediately you have sold something.
- The likelihood is that the product you are selling on behalf of somebody else is a simpler, lower-price sale. Might not the time taken to make such sales detract from the time available to speak to potential customers of your main business? If it does, you have a resource problem. You need more staff in the shop, and you cannot get them in packages of less than one. If you need only a half a one, you are paying for an awful lot of magazine-reading time.
- If you solve the staff problem by allowing the new supplier to be in charge from time to time, you hit the problem already discussed – they cannot sell your product because you are the product and you are not there.

The message from the front line is clear. Stick with what you know and make your dream work. Don't get involved in someone else's.

Idea 72 – Tick again

A healthy business has a strong pulse, but you need to be able to count it. It is true that profitability is an important measure of the health of your dream business. It is out of profits that you pay yourself and it is out of profits that you fund increases in stock and the general growth of the business. But profits without cash are like a shop window with cardboard cakes in it. It looks nice, but there is nothing you can do with it. Here is a simple example of a shop whose profitability is unquestionable, but whose cash position does not just threaten its ability to pay dividends, but also its ability to survive.

The shop is making a healthy profit. In fact its return on capital employed at 20% is pretty good. There is nothing untoward either about its ability to pay its interest charges out of its profits. In fact interest accounts for less than a third of its profits before interest and tax. Here are the numbers:

Long term debt	60.0
Shareholders' funds	40.0
Capital employed	100.0
Return on capital employed	20%
Profit before interest and tax	20.0
Interest rate	10%
Interest	6.0
Profit before tax	14.0
Tax rate	25%
Tax	3.5
Net profit after interest and tax	10.5

Unfortunately those numbers only show one of the implications of debt i.e. interest. Another one is making repayments. In this case the company has to pay back £12,000 a year on the five-year loan. Now look at the numbers:

Net profit after interest and tax (as before)	10.5
Repayments	12.0
Net cash outflow	-1.5

So, bad luck, they are making money and running out of cash. The great idea is that you keep a constant running cashflow up to date. Whenever a significant transaction takes place, map it on to your cashflow. Before you spend money, even although it is on stock or other necessary investment, see what it will do for your cashflow. Don't miss anything out. A mistake in predicting your profitability may give you a problem in the medium term; but you can deal with that because you have time to correct it. A problem with your cash is instant and lethal. Banks hate surprises. Your relationship with them will be healthy if they are confident that you have your finger on the pulse of your business – particularly the pulse that counts the cash. So TICK – *think in cash, knucklehead.*

Idea 73 – First run a pilot

In managing any project that involves change, most project managers find it advisable to run a pilot. This is good advice for the small businessperson as well. If you are going to sell a new line or go nationwide with an idea, think of some way that you can test the water with a pilot before rolling it out to a full implementation.

As an entrepreneur you can do this with entire businesses. A good example of this is in a high-tech one where a successful person created a new business with the minimum resources possible, a manager and a tightly knit team. In the team were, say, a couple of sales people, a technical guru and someone for customer administration and support. This team then runs the micro business pretty much as though it were their own. They identify and sort out the problems, make it a success and teach you how the model works. You can then roll it out knowing the viability of the model and the financials. The technique is also brilliant for giving confidence to investors if you need them for the roll out.

Ten Greatest Quick Tips for Building the Dream

Introduction

If you talk to successful dream builders, they will all come up with their list of tips. Some require no explanation; some need some additions to the one-liner to get the point over. All have stood the test of time and represent good advice to the novice dreamer.

Idea 74 – Don't let today's mail set today's agenda

A large business can turn a small business on its head with one phone call. You get a call, for example, from BT asking if you would be interested in quoting for a training course that will eventually be rolled out to all Level 3 staff, a huge number of people. 'You are in a bit late, actually, because I did not know of you until I spoke to one of the target audience who said he had attended one of your courses when working for another company. Sorry to put pressure on, but I need to brief you in the next couple of days and get your proposal within a week.' What do you say?

Most people will drop everything for such an opportunity, and on some occasions they would be right to do so – which makes the decision less than straightforward. In most cases, going from experience they would be wrong. The individual making the request is a training person – so you have no contact with top management. Existing competitors are driving the timescale. You only have the word of a past candidate that you can understand and meet the need. And so it goes on. It takes real courage to turn such an opportunity down, but almost certainly it is the right thing to do. Do it positively, of course, saying that this is not the right time for you to meet such strict timescales, and that the speed with which they are acting gives you less than enough time to react to the best of your ability, and so on. Give good reasons for not going for this one and then ask to meet the person at a later date to discuss their requirements for future projects and make sure you get the name of the person who recommended you so that you can go and see them as well.

The result of such 'positive qualifying out' will be an opportunity to get into BT in the future, and also a clear signal whether or not your proposal would be taken seriously. If the training manager remonstrates with you insisting that the recommender had painted a picture of your training that was an exact fit for their requirement, then reluctantly and modestly you can change your mind. If they just say 'OK, thank you for your frankness', you probably did the right thing.

This is one specific case to illustrate this first tip. Somehow you have got to get to a stage where there is a plan and you are sticking to it – flexibly of course. Another angle on this is when the owners of the business become so bogged down in the running of the administration and office work that they never get out to the customers. You need discipline here to block out in the diary an increasing amount of time when you will be out 'doing it' and then stick to that plan.

Idea 75 – Know your critical success factors

OK, I don't much like the term either, but it says exactly what you need to do. Sit down and work out what you need to get right in order to exist now and in the future. Some critical success factors (CSFs) will be common to your industry, and you can read them up; others will be peculiar to your offering and only you can identify them. One of your CSFs is also known as your USP – Unique Selling Proposition or propositions. Anyway, find them out, tell people about them, work hard on them and review them from time to time because nothing stays still.

Idea 76 – Don't expand too quickly

Your meticulous cash management should stop you from getting into a syndrome called 'overtrading', where the expansion of your business goes too fast for your cashflow and people resources. Look, it is very likely that you are in it for the long haul, so take it easy. Steady growth will get there better than explosive growth if that threatens the foundations of the business.

Idea 77 – Concentrate on what you are good at …

Reputation and word of mouth are the greatest marketing assets you can have. Encourage this by sticking to your core business. Wide-angled guesses at a new opportunity just because you have some cash in the bank can be an expensive mistake. You have a new learning curve to go up, and your competition is likely to be at least one step ahead. Perhaps the best clue is the old adage whereby it is a good idea to take an old product into a new market in terms of diversification, or a new product into an old market. Taking new products into new markets is often a step too far.

Idea 78 – … But don't ignore opportunities to reduce risk

On the other hand, there are some major benefits to diversification. It tends to reduce risk by making you less vulnerable to a market suddenly collapsing or the introduction of a competitive product that makes life in this particular product market difficult – temporarily or permanently. Especially under this heading, try not to get over-exposed to one customer. It takes only a change of personnel, or a move by a competitor, to damage your business with a single client. The most frequent rule of thumb I have heard, and used myself, is that no customer should give you more than half of your turnover two years running. Another is to keep all customers below 33% of your sales at any time.

Idea 79 – Sell to your existing customers

There are those in the know who say that it costs seven times as much to sell products or services to a new prospect as it does to sell the same products and services to an existing customer. This is particularly true of those customers who are big, say international, businesses. Work the corridors. Ask your current clients for the names of other people in the organisation who could also benefit from your services. This is worth an awful lot:

- You may be the first in to speak to someone about a new opportunity.
- A recommendation from someone the new prospect respects is worth its weight in gold.
- Your product or service will probably require little alteration to meet the new need. This gives you a good gross margin.
- You are moving towards becoming the company standard that makes selling even easier.
- Your top management contacts give you good leverage, see *Idea 49*.

If the customer is an American company and you can get exposure and orders in the USA, you have just opened up a market the size of which you hitherto only dreamed about.

Idea 80 – Don't buy a mobile phone

This is a tricky one. Most people running a business have a mobile phone to 'keep in touch'. But don't forget two things. First of all people built the business of their dreams fifteen years ago without the aid of mobile phones. The thing you will have least of is thinking time, and mobile phones spell the end to that. Two hours on a train thinking about how you are doing and where you are going will in many cases be much more valuable to the business than the ability of your people to give you a problem that, if they had been unable to contact you, they might very well have been able to solve themselves.

In a meeting yesterday a senior manager in a telecommunications firm told me how one day he had spent the whole of a three-hour train journey on the phone. He switched it off to attend the meeting he was going to and when he came out there were 17 voice mail messages. There is something very wrong there and the mobile phone is hiding the symptoms of an organisational and delegation problem that could cost him or his business dear. It could cost the business dear if he makes a mistake by being too thinly spread; and I hope he is making lots of money so that his widow will be comfortable when he has his heart attack.

If you cannot imagine life without a mobile phone, try it for a week. You may have to switch it on again the next week, but you will have discovered the virtue of being out of touch for some periods of time.

If you cannot imagine life without a mobile phone, try it for a week. You may have to switch it on again the next week, but you will have discovered the virtue of being out of touch for some periods of time.

Idea 81 – Don't become obsessed with saving tax

Remember that if you give the Government 40% of your profits, then you have kept 60%. You can waste a lot of time saving tax, and if you cut corners and get a full investigation started you can wave goodbye to an immense amount of your and your accountant's time and your money.

Some years ago I worked in the Edinburgh office of a business whose head office was in London. One of my colleagues had organised a payment of bonus, quite legally, that reduced the tax burden by spreading the payments over two tax years. Then the administrators blew it and paid the whole lot at once. The phone lines between Edinburgh became hot and the language ripe, as he tried to sort it out. He made good progress but had not 100% restored the planned position. I swear he took the next two days arguing and fighting for his rights. We calculated that the last one and a half days concerned the last and smallest item, and made a difference to him after tax of less than £10 in today's money. There must have been something better he could have done with that time.

The very serious side of this is that managers can look at a decision that makes complete sense in every way except tax and have to drop the idea. On the other hand, wrong decisions driven by avoiding tax could be costly.

Idea 82 – Don't dream your way into stupid projects

Sometimes our dreams are really prejudices and ill-conceived desires. I know a consultant who lost a major customer because he bought a Ferrari just after the customer had helped him out of a cash flow problem.

When the fashion is to buy, prices go high. At the top of the economic cycle there are many temptations to pay too much for a company, for the head office building or for the annual kick-off meeting in the Bahamas. An old mentor of mine used to say that if a company built a new head office building with fountains and a helicopter pad and then got the Duke of Edinburgh to open it – run like hell. He regarded this as a sure sign of trouble just round the corner.

Keep your feet on the ground and stick to the knitting.

Idea 83 – Learn from the mistakes of others

This could be combined with 'If your instincts say it is wrong, it is probably wrong.' If you see something going pear shaped in another business and realise that you are acting in a similar way, then change things. History in business does repeat itself and there are loads of cautionary tales from which we can all learn.

Six Greatest Ideas for Building Creative Plans

Introduction

To attain your dream, you have to keep dreaming. The problem this gives you is to bridge the dream into a creative plan where the output is what you and your team are actually going to do. Most successful people have found this out and arranged for themselves and their board and other teams of people to go off site to produce a plan. For this you need a process – the creative planning process. All planning processes include three elements – analysis, objective setting and activity planning. *Idea 85* illustrates this in a particular circumstance – building the account plan you need in order to maintain and expand your biggest customers. I use this one as an illustration because it has the element of analysing the customer position as well as your own. You can use the same process equally well, with only minor alterations, for building a creative business plan.

So, it's not optional, get the people who need to be there together and build a creative plan.

Idea 84 – Of course we will always keep our biggest customers ... (not)

This idea and the next one are mainly concerned with the sellers of complex products building the business of their dreams by selling high quantities of products and services to other businesses, particularly to large businesses with long chains of command. You may sell heating and ventilation systems to contractors, for example, or fast-moving consumer goods to supermarkets. Another contender for this treatment is consultancy, be it management consultancy or recruitment for example. The key is that you are a selling team, and that you are selling to a buying team. It is, of course, a logical extension of big ticket selling, but this is the joined-up version where you are active in a key account all the time, continuously taking orders from them and always in some way involved in delivering or implementing what you have sold.

Key account customers for many businesses supply 80% of the orders taken in any one year. The loss of any of them causes problems, the loss of the biggest or more than one of the others could be catastrophic. (BNFL in 2000 claimed to have some 30 customers and therefore to be secure despite losing all their Japanese business. The Japanese business just happened to put into the shade all the other customers put together.)

So we need a system or business process that monitors and ensures customer satisfaction and, at the same time, builds the overall relationship and finds new opportunities preferable before the competition.

The position of BNFL is not uncommon. It is easy to become too dependent on one customer. After all it is much easier to make sales to people who know you, and finding a new prospect in the same organisation takes much less effort than finding a new customer altogether. And, by definition, the key account is pleased with you. Your business processes are in synchronisation, regular delivery means that your people and theirs are working in familiar areas and so on.

Indeed some companies become too dependent on a small number of customers because the customer is delighted to assist in making this happen. Their negotiating position becomes better and better, whilst, although the short term may show larger profits, the supplying company's negotiating position is becoming worse and worse. Even if there is absolutely no malice aforethought, the world changes and a big-company strategy that has worked for many years can suddenly go phut. Think about Marks and Spencer who carried their buy-British strategy on for so long that their share price crashed and their leading directors left to spend more time with their families. The effect on those who depended too much on them was catastrophic.

As I said before, I cannot really find any scientific evidence for what constitutes becoming too dependent, but a rule of thumb that I have used seems to get good acceptance from the people I have discussed it with. This is, don't get more than 33% of any year's revenue from a single account.

Idea 85 – Use a good planning process

So, you have a small number of key accounts and, let us say, an account manager responsible for them. You need to get the manager and team to produce a plan to ensure and exploit that long-term relationship. The 'bible' of the account manager is the key account plan, or whatever you choose to call it. The you in the rest of this idea is the account manager who may, of course, be you – the owner of the business.

Planning mission

A planning session starts from a vision or mission. We want to change, possibly dramatically, a part of the world to our vision of it. The mission could be very broad or very focused; but it gives the starting point of the plan.

The objective of a planning session is 'to produce the best possible plan to achieve this mission'. Notice how the objective breaks the rules of normal objectives – 'best possible' is not an accurate measurement for achievement. We have to accept this though, as a more accurate test for success could constrain the creative thinking of the plan.

Examples of planning team mission statements could look like this:

- to be the supplier of first choice to the account in all of Europe and North America;
- to be and to be seen to be a major supplier in the civil government market;

- to improve our market share in the account worldwide;
- to achieve at least ten per cent higher level of revenue growth in the account every year for the next three years; and
- to use our reputation in the pharmaceuticals division of the customer to gain ten per cent of the orders placed in the chemicals division within a year.

Who is there?

The planning team should include most of the people who will be involved with the implementation of the plan. The account manager, any technical support person and possibly a marketing person may be appropriate.

If there is a facilitator, he or she will be responsible for describing and getting agreement to the ground rules of planning. He or she will also police and time the session to ensure that by the end the team has reached an appropriate point in the process.

It is highly desirable for you or another senior manager to attend the last session of the key account planning event to hear a short presentation of the team's conclusions. This gives a focus to the team who will have to be ready to make such a presentation when the time comes.

How long do you work?

If your plan is concerned with a limited part of the customer's business, you should be able to put a plan together within a day. Bigger teams with bigger tasks could take a lot more. By the way, experience shows that after eight or nine hours the productivity of planners drops dramatically. It is probably better, therefore, to finish at around 17.30. If it is a new team or some new members are joining, it is a good idea to have the meeting off-site and to have dinner together. Don't forget, though, you are trying to make these planning events regular and routine. It is a good idea to call a one- or two-day planning session to modify a particular part of the plan and to hold such a meeting in an ordinary conference room.

The documentation of a planning session should be on flip charts subsequently transferred to an electronic file.

The creative planning process

The word 'creative' reminds us that we are looking for the best possible plan. Try to avoid all your prejudices and preconceived ideas. In particular, in the early part of the planning process do not constrain your thinking by doubts about the availability of resources.

We will of course recognise that there is a management budgeting cycle and that each plan needs to have resources approved at appropriate times during that cycle.

Nevertheless we need creative ideas to generate new initiatives. After all, any company's management can put resources where they like. If the team gives management a good business case and enough time to react, you may have to buy in resources seeing from the plan the results that will follow.

The creative planning process has various steps, described below.

Gather a database of knowledge
Remember the Chinese proverb – do not decide where you want to go and how to get there until you are quite certain where you are now.

The team needs to understand the customer's business, the customer's industry, the customer's current financial and competitive environment, the influences of the general economy, etc.

That's before the team adds the supplier–company environment, its current market strategies, position in the account, products and services, etc. If we have organised a huge database of knowledge, planning will become more and more effective.

For the moment let us imagine that, either before or during the event, the account manager has briefed the planning team on the information necessary to take part in the creation of the plan.

In one very large privatised business the organisation chart did not reveal – without further examination – the fact that many established and up-and-coming executives had not only attended the same university, but also the same college.

The team will never have all the facts at its fingertips. Indeed in a new account penetration plan there will be little information to hand and the planning session will be quite short, but the more information available to the team the better.

Soft data is in many ways as important or even more important than hard data. It includes all the prejudices and politics of the people side of the business. This data consists of the subjective views of customer managers or the account team.

Do not take things at face value. In any large company there is an organisation chart. It contains hard data such as, 'That person reports to that person, who reports to that person, who reports to that person, etc'.

The soft data asks, 'Yes, but who actually runs the business, who has influence, who can make things happen and equally – who can stop things happening?'

In many large British companies there is a network of people with similar backgrounds who, though in different divisions and at different levels in the business, form a powerful *virtual team*.

In one very large privatised business the organisation chart did not reveal – without further examination – the fact that many established and up-and-coming executives had not only attended the same university, but also the same college within the university.

The environment section of a creative planning process includes the background knowledge including the soft data brought by everyone in the team.

Analyse this data
The analysis technique for sorting out your knowledge and different team members'

angles on the plan is called SWOT analysis – *s*trengths, *w*eaknesses, *o*pportunities and *t*hreats.

This is a simple technique, as so many good ones are, for helping the team to understand what it needs to do in the account.

Unfortunately, like all techniques it can be implemented well and therefore also badly. Suffice it to say that a comprehensive, well-documented SWOT analysis makes the next part of the planning process reasonably straightforward.

The objective of SWOT analysis is not simply to describe the environment; rather it is to describe the environment in a way that helps us to understand what we need to do.

It is in two parts, the customer SWOT (C-SWOT) and the supplier SWOT (S-SWOT).

Once you have an agreed description of the environment, you can decide what to do about it.

Set the objectives for the team
Following the use of a bridging technique to ensure that the work done in the SWOT analysis is fully exploited, *Idea 87*, the team sets its goals.

In a key account plan, goals are divided into account management goals and sales campaign goals.

Account management goals are the relationship goals and tend to be more strategic and longer term than campaign goals. Experience has enabled professional account managers to break down account management goals into eight goal areas.

Not all plans will require goals in all eight areas, but all plans will require goals in some of these areas. The detail of this follows in *Idea 88*, but for the sake of example, three of these goal areas are:

- level of contact;
- customer satisfaction; and
- market share.

Campaign goals are goals where a major milestone is taking an order from a customer for the supplier's products and/or services. The methods used for campaign planning are explained in *Idea 52*.

Having decided what you want to achieve, you get to the last part of the planning process – the activity plans.

Plan the activities necessary to achieve the objectives

It is very much a personal decision as to the amount of detail into which activity plans have to go. Some people are comfortable with quite macro actions and milestones that are weeks or even months apart. Other people try to plan all the activities required to achieve the objective in the minutest detail, even down to a telephone call.

It is personal preference. Either will do if it achieves the aim of activity planning which is to estimate the resources required to achieve the objective.

The team should now be in a position to produce its best forecast of its achievements in the account both short and long term and the amount of resource investment required from the supplying company to achieve these results.

Re-sort the activity plan into a resource plan

The resource plan is actually a re-sort of the activity plan. If you know what has to be done and who has to do it, you can produce your best estimate of the resources required.

This enables us to move to the next step in the planning process. This is either part of the normal budgeting cycle or on some occasions a special case to take to management as a long- or short-term business investment plan.

It is vital to narrow down accurate definition of the resources that will implement the plan. Too often the team starts to implement the early part of the plan, only to find a resource problem later.

The team needs to get itself into good order to move to the next step, which is to persuade management to put those resources at the team's disposal.

Get agreement to the allocation of the resources to implement the plan
Most account plans require resources not in the direct control of the account team. A decision box occurs therefore when management decide on the merits of the various plans being put forward and allocate their resources.

Try to see this as a contract. The account team is saying to management 'I will give you these results [objectives] if you will give me these resources.' If management say 'yes', either immediately or as the budgeting cycle grinds on, the team implements the plan.

If management say no, the team adjusts its goals and resubmits because, of course, no planning process is complete until the resources have been allocated to its implementation.

Be careful. Management can often from their wider experience offer short cuts towards account teams' objectives and therefore legitimately reduce the amount of resource required to achieve the result.

However, in an immature planning cycle, management, particularly sales management, have a habit of liking the sound of the result, but not allocating the resource in full.

At worst this leads to teams second-guessing the likelihood of their getting resources when they are setting goals, and completely constrains the creativity of the plan.

For their part, account teams must recognise that while management can get any resource required to achieve a well-constructed business plan, it requires more than a week's notice. The plans must signal in detail this year's resource requirement and broadly the requirement of the subsequent two years, particularly if special or unusual resources are going to be required.

Idea 86 – Get the team to toe the line

Any planning team needs to obey some ground rules concerned with the efficiency of the planning session. Where two or three people are gathered together, you will find differences of opinion, multiple ideas, different angles on the same topic, personal prejudices and all the other features of a team of human beings.

These tend to reduce the efficiency of a team. It is the job of the facilitator and of course of the team itself, to maintain a number of disciplines.

Talk and document in short, simple but complete sentences

This item is proved in the detail on SWOT analysis, and is probably the most important rule. If we talk in bullet points then we will get quick agreement to a rough definition of the key issues. But, what we need is the agreement of the team to a detailed statement of the *real meaning* of the key issue.

Equal voice, equal vote.

In a creative planning session, rank disappears. It is vital that the planning team does not believe that it is there to wait until the senior person has expressed a view and then agree with it.

Real creativity may easily come from a member of the team who is the most junior and therefore the least experienced. So, chief executives and account managers, a sure way to kill the creativity of your team is to make it plain, after about an hour of planning, that the only plan which is going to be acceptable is the one you had in your head before the meeting started.

Remember that to get a team committed to a plan of action you must encourage it to take part in the planning process. Avoid telling them what they are going to do, like a prophet with tablets of stone.

In the end however, the team has to get to a plan. The difference between equal voice and equal vote is best shown by an example. In a discussion about where to go on holiday children have an equal voice, they can say where they want to go, but they certainly don't have a vote.

The account manager's neck is on the block, so in extreme cases he or she may have to use some assertiveness to get to a satisfactory conclusion. In practice there are rarely problems in this area. The team is pleased to be part of the planning process and will normally get amicably to the necessary consensus.

100 per cent agreement

Allied to the above is the rule of 100 per cent agreement. Read literally this means that no part of the plan is firm until all members of the team have agreed with it.

It is important. Most planning sessions produce new directions and new activities for all of the members of the team. In many cases these will be in addition to or different from the activities which the team member has underway.

If the momentum of the plan is to be kept up and the new directions implemented, it is vital that everyone agrees and that the timescales and resources have been accurately forecast.

If this rule goes wrong, you will find that people are not disagreeing with a part of the plan only because they have in fact no intention of carrying out their role in it. 'They can write it up if they want, it ain't going to happen.'

Do not duck issues

Following on the 100 per cent agreement, a successful planning session tables and discusses all the key issues surrounding the plan. Here are some examples of issues that are frequently ducked.

- A person agrees to an activity, but team members do not believe he or she has the necessary knowledge or skills to carry it out.
- A necessary activity is in someone else's province and we duck the issue of how to get that person's buy-in to the plan.
- An activity is agreed which depends on higher management agreement and no plan is put in place to gain this.
- An activity is agreed which depends on the customer, and no plan is put in place to ensure that the customer can and does achieve the dependency.

Think before you speak

Don't stick to this too rigidly because sometimes people do think through an idea while they are articulating it. But it is a useful rule to agree before the planning session starts so that we can use it to muffle someone who frequently waffles.

The facilitator will present these rules to the team and, given that they agree to abide by them, the planning session proper can begin.

Idea 87 – Connect analysis to objectives tightly

A lot of planning sessions fail because the planners find it impossible to get their brains round a good and detailed analysis and produce objectives that reflect it. You need at this point a neat bridging mechanism to act as a connector between the SWOT analysis and the plan itself. Without this simple device it is very difficult to get a good link, and basically to know where to start.

You need one other ingredient. *Idea 75* mentioned the importance of understanding your critical success factors. Write these down in the left column of a matrix with five columns. Now number the strengths, weaknesses, opportunities and threats. This is nothing to do with priorities; it is simply a mechanism for identifying each element of the analysis section. In the example, the weaknesses numbered 1, 8, 9, 17 and 23 are the ones the plan will need to eliminate if it is to be strong in CSF 1.

Now under the SWOT headings transfer each item on to the matrix. It will look like this:

Goal area	Remove weaknesses	Exploit opportunities	Avoid threats	Use strengths
Critical success factor 1	1,8,9,17,23	3,4,8,9,14	1,3,4	1,3,4,6,8,12
Critical success factor 2	2,3,7,15,16	1,2,5	2,6,10	2,4,6,8,10,
Critical success factor 3	20,21,22	6,10,11,12	7,8,11	1,3,4,7,8,9
Critical success factor 4	4,5,6,10,11,12	7,13	5,9	2,8,9,12
Critical success factor 5	1,17,24	16		2,7,8,9,11
Critical success factor 6	13,14,18,19,20	15	12,13	13,14
Critical success factor 7	25,27	19,22	14,15	9,11,13
Critical success factor 8	26,28,29	17,18,20,21	16	2,8,12,13

Obey this rule if possible – *allocate a weakness, opportunity or threat to only one goal area.* We are getting near allocating responsibility for the achievement of progress in the plan to individuals. Each W, O and T will probably represent a milestone in the activity plan. It is important therefore that no action falls between two people's responsibilities. Hence the rule.

When it comes to strengths, we may of course put each strength into as many goal areas as possible. At action-planning time, the team will use the strengths as pointers to what they can exploit to eliminate weaknesses.

Idea 88 – Use radar again

You get a good view of your strengths and weaknesses if you use a radar diagram to reflect your progress against your critical success factors. As an illustration, here are some common critical success factors for a key customer, along with examples of why you would score yourself as shown:

1. *Level of contact – score 3*
   We have never spoken to top management at corporate level. In the Division where we are strong we have slumped to a project manager level with the division's general manager meeting us only socially from time to time.

2. *Customer satisfaction – score 6*
   We have performed well and score highly on the customer satisfaction survey. We do not have detailed information of the real business benefits our products have given them.

3. *Account planning – score 2*
   We have hardly started this and are blocked from getting the process going by our poor level of contact.

4. *Competitive position – score 8*
   It would take a very long time indeed to get rid of our installed base. They are pretty dependent on us

5. *Strategic applications, products and services – score 6*
   We know that what we provide should be strategic, but we do not really know how to exploit this.

6. *Customer strategies – score 7*
   Our knowledge of the customer's strategy gives us confidence that our products and services will continue to be important to them.

7. *Prospecting – score 5*
   Our pipeline of prospects is not sufficient to reflect our market share. We do not understand the opportunities at corporate or divisional level outside the one division where we are strong.

8. *Market share – score 5*
   Our market share has just increased significantly and will continue to do so in the short term as the new projects are implemented. The key to maintaining that momentum is to discover more opportunities in the pipeline.

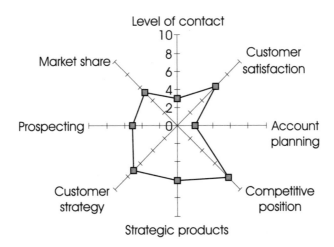

Idea 89 – Keep the documentation brief

One of the many reasons people are put off making creative plans occurs if you require them to write screeds of data on volumes of forms. The essential part of a plan is simply:

- the list of critical success factors;
- the spider's web;
- for each objective an activity plan on one page.

The plan should therefore only have about 10 pages, and most people can handle that.

Eight Greatest Ideas for Growing by Acquisition

Introduction

So far we have mainly concentrated on building the business of your dreams through internal growth. The dream starts to loom larger quicker when you look at the process of taking over going concerns. There is no reason if you have applied KISS, *keep it simple stupid*, and built your business by trading ('If you do that, I will do this'), why you cannot take this into making deals and forming bigger companies by trading businesses or divisions of businesses. It can look frightening, *think big, unimaginably big Idea 91*, but it uses the same common sense and awareness of approach that has got you this far. So here are the greatest ideas for building your dream in large lumps, courtesy of four inveterate deal makers.

Idea 90 – Treat big organisations as a collection of individuals

If you are involved with big organisations because you are organising a management buyout or attempting to take over a part of their business, you must treat them as individuals not as a sensible or logical institution. If we take *ease yourself out by MBO Idea 5* a step further you will see what I mean. The profitability of an internal division is measured by the management accounting system. This has to include its making a contribution to all the overheads of parts of the business above it, such as head office. Given that fact, try this test. Think of the objections that a manager might come up with to your leaving the business and buying out a small portion of it. You will be involved in a sales campaign even though the objective is to buy something – so think through the objections from their point of view.

If your first thought was, 'Well they will have to find somewhere else to apportion the costs that used to be apportioned to the part of the business I am buying, or cut back on some overhead expense', you are not treating the organisation as a collection of individuals. That objection is completely logical but may very well not cross the decision-maker's mind. Think, therefore, about the decision maker. How will this deal affect his or her performance this year? Is there some way that this deal will improve his or her performance against their key indicators? It has been known for a deal to be struck which did not do the selling company much good, but which enabled the managers responsible for the unit being sold to meet their profit targets for the year. That is, they were able to take into their profits all of the income stemming from the one-off phenomenon of disposing of an asset. Yes, I know it's no way to run a business but that is how it is often done.

Remember also that a lot of middle and quite senior managers have no responsibility at all for cashflow. This can be very helpful as you trade an improvement in their putative profit position (an opinion) for an improvement in your cashflow (reality). Delaying a sum of money passing from you to them may not be against their interests at all, while it may be the difference between life and death to you. Conversely, money coming in up-front is worth a whole lot more than money in a year's time to you but makes precious little difference to a middle manager's ability to shine.

Now think about the staffing side from their point of view. The thing the managers will miss more than the business you are buying is *you*. So start working on this objection at an early stage. You should already have been grooming the likely person to take over from you. You will have been modestly talking him or her up for a while before the exit negotiations start. Send them to the international conference in your place – remember you do not need the high profile but they will if they are to be seen as a seamless transition into your job when you leave. Get this wrong and you could have an implacable, not to say scared, manager trying to hold on to the division you wish to buy only because they cannot imagine life without you.

Next pay some attention to corporate hot buttons. At any time there are some parameters that large organisations are trying to change. When you say something to a middle manager that rings a bell with one of these parameters, you have hit that manager's hot button. Concentrate your effort on acquisitions that do this. Ask yourself the question, 'What deal could I do with this person that will end up with him or her getting a new feather in their cap by making a change in an area the company is focused on?'

Ask yourself the question, 'What deal could I do with this person that will end up with him or her getting a new feather in their cap by making a change in an area the company is focused on?'

Idea 91 – Think big, unimaginably big

Let us assume for a moment that you are a small business with some substance but still demonstrably a small business. Can I also assume that you are in a niche market that you understand entirely and where you have found ways of getting competitive edge and prospering? Now think about your largest competitor, that is the company that in the niche is the market leader at least by volume. Now ask yourself 'Would life be easier if these people did not exist or were on our side?' It is more likely that you could make this happen by taking that part of the business over if it is not making money, but even if it is, anything is possible.

Now look at how strategic this part of the business is to its current owners. Could it be described, even if it is profitable, as non-strategic? I know a small company that bought the division of a big company because strategically it was trying to get out of the software business. (Incidentally, the big business did not really know if the division was making money or not.) Analyse who is in charge of the business at middle-management level or just above. Could you approach them directly, or would you need an adviser to make the first move?

You will quickly see whether you can make such a business pay; then go back to finding the hot button that makes a manager want to sell no matter what the impact on the overall business is. The final point to remember is that you must think big, because there is nothing a manager in a large organisation will not do to make his or her name.

Idea 92 – Make sure your people are aiming in the same direction as you

Sensible businesspeople must learn another lesson from the two ideas above. If it is possible to make a good acquisition by treating employees of big organisations as individuals and not treating the corporation as a logical entity, the same can happen to you as you build the business of your dreams. Don't fall into this trap. Look carefully and frequently at the incentives and motivations you have in place for your staff. Is there anything in terms of career advancement, money or other reward that could induce your people to work in a way that was against the interests of the business and your objectives? If there is, fix it.

The trick is to come back to your objectives. If your objective is to build the biggest then set targets aimed at achieving this. If your objective is to make money fast and get out when the going is good, then set different targets. It is as simple, or outrageously difficult, as that.

Idea 93 – Don't economise on tax advice

We have talked before about the importance of negotiating with everyone including your friendly professionals such as accountants and lawyers. Here is one further illustration. A company was offered £1 million by a venture capital company for 33% of the shares. The owners went to another company and through competitive negotiation got a second offer of the £1 million this time for only 20% of the share capital.

Another popular way of going about a takeover that reduces the downside risk of the thing not happening is to negotiate what are sometimes called 'contingent fees'. You pay only if the deal comes off.

Don't, however, stint on tax advice when discussing and making bids for businesses. You cannot ever know enough about tax unless you dedicate yourself to it entirely; so buy it in.

They will tell you about disposals through stock dividends, things to do prior to the sale of a business, bonus dividends of shares and multiple other ways of ensuring that you do not pay more tax than your activities warrant.

It came home to me in another way the other day, when a friend of mine was talking about filing for probate for his father's estate. The estate, mainly because of the property involved, had to pay inheritance tax. This made a huge difference to the amount of time and effort required to make a settlement with the tax office that was appropriate for both parties – taxed and taxers. With inheritance tax at your marginal rate, say 40%, you need to put in the time.

It's the same in business although not so personally immediate and clear cut.

Idea 94 – Plan bottom-up as well as top-down

We have given some space to planning top-down. Here is a bit of advice from a serial takeover specialist. 'When you have done your top-down plan, present it to the managers below and get them to put the detail into it. The devil is indeed in the detail. This does two important things. Firstly it is a good, practical sanity check on the viability of the plan, secondly it enables you to spot the problem areas when things go wrong.'

Idea 95 – Take care with fair value adjustments

You will need to understand the 'whys and wherefores' of this. Fundamentally, when you take over a new company you will be under pressure to produce profits quickly. You have to make sure that not only are you not fighting with one arm tied behind your back, but also that you start off a bit ahead of the game.

Due to differences in accounting policies between the two companies, you will make fair value adjustments in many areas including sales revenues and product cost. Don't forget the element of risk. You may be able to adjust values in your favour if there is a risk, for example, of late delivery of a significant order.

There are many innovative ways of structuring businesses. Look for them. You can get off the balance sheet, for example, with preference shares and then convert them to ordinary shares through a call option. Remember profit is an opinion; so make sure you can sell the opinion most conducive to your objectives.

Idea 96 – Don't bet the firm

It was the popular opinion of most of the people I discussed this issue with that you should not have to take huge risks to build your dream. You have to take a sensible time target, and informed and controlled risks. One said to me, 'Don't get your company into a situation where a single event could put you down unless you really cannot avoid it. Be prepared to bet the business, but don't plan to do it. After all, if that situation does occur you have disobeyed an important planning rule – always have a fall-back contingency plan.'

Idea 97 – Buy the underpants of your dreams

The takeover or merger of two companies reaches a mad rush crescendo of work just before the deed is done. One of the family mottos of the impresario Grade family is, 'If you want an answer today, the answer is no.' Up to a point, Lord Grade. In the takeover business an answer tomorrow is too late. So work hard and fast.

In this regard two entrepreneurs who had worked together for a while gave an unusual demonstration of the totally complementary skills and attitudes that had made their partnership so successful. At the end of a particularly difficult deal they were cloistered with their legal and financial advisers all night. To allow them to face the new day with no sleep they needed to freshen up and change their underwear and shirts. One of them went out to buy these and came back with Marks and Spencer goods to the value of less than £55 for the two of them.

Some months later the same situation occurred with another deal. The other of the two went shopping this time and came back having shopped at Gucci; total cost – the thick edge of £150. But what the hell, he had the underpants of his dreams.

Three Greatest Ideas for Building the Empire of Your Dreams

Introduction

For whatever reason, many people find that their dream does not lie in their own business. They like the comfort of an employer, and the security of a company car and pension scheme. But into middle age, even these people start to feel that 'Yes, but what is in it for me?' feeling of those who, at that time of life, take the plunge.

There is, of course, a middle road. Build your own empire within an empire. Run your part of the business in such a way that you become as autonomous as you wish. Perhaps you could make your division into a separate subsidiary company, this gives you many of the trappings of going on your own, even including share options linked to the performance of your company. Here are three ideas for pursuing that dream.

Do not mislead yourself; empire-building is not a part-time job; so the first thing you have to do is make your department or division run using very little of your time.

Idea 98 – Get someone else to do the work

Do not mislead yourself – empire-building is not a part-time job – so the first thing you have to do is make your department or division run using very little of your time. This is particularly true if you are in a location remote from head office where empire-type decisions are made. You will need to be there much more than back at the ranch; so make sure you have someone good whom you can trust to run the operational side of the business without you.

I know that this has some dangers, not the least of which is that any person good enough to fulfil this role will realise that he or she is actually producing the results. They will manoeuvre this situation towards their own career ambitions and this could threaten your comfortable position. This is unavoidable. Look after them well and only let them go for a good promotion so that the next person in will think of their next progress being outside the division rather than toppling you.

Idea 99 – Take on extraneous tasks

Empire builders need a very high profile with senior managers. A key way to achieving this is to volunteer for tasks that need to be done but which are not strictly within your ambit. Obviously avoid the poisoned chalices that lurk in every board minute, but look for opportunities to make a high-profile contribution to the sponsorship programme, or the new technology project or whatever.

Don't just look for them – invent them. Research some changes that are occurring in your marketplace and put up a paper identifying the challenge and suggesting how to take the matter forward, and who should do the taking (probably you). Your objective is to be as knowledgeable about the rest of the company as you are of your own bit. Fame and stardom should follow.

Idea 100 – Read a book about it

These two ideas and 98 others are more fully discussed in *The 100 Greatest Ideas for Building Your Career*, Langdon, Capstone and WHSmith, 2000.

Contributors of Ideas

Alan Bonham
Andy Bruce
Graham McKenzie-Washington
John Harris
John Wood, Glenhurst Ltd
John Wright
Mark Allin
Nick Wenman
Penny Ariff
Phil Magree
Richard Burton
Richard Humphreys
Roger Hennah (winner of the bottle of champagne)
Ros Jay
Stephen Waters

Index